The Beginner's Guide to Intermittent Keto

High-Fat Low-Carb
Recipes

Author
Delores D. Ritchie

Contents

INTRODUCTION TO INTERMITTENT FASTING AND THE KETO DIET IN PART I

CHANGING FOR THE BETTER HEALTH

What we consume makes us who we are. Doesn't it seem like a clear, straightforward statement? But let's take it a step further and think about how we consume. If you're reading this book, you're probably searching for a change. Maybe the objective is to reduce weight, to get rid of those final 10 pounds. Perhaps you're thinking of altering your diet as a preventative step to set yourself on a healthier path in the future.

Since you purchased this book in the first place, you're undoubtedly acquainted with the phrases intermittent fasting and ketosis, commonly known as IF and Keto. Unlike fad diets, which promise quick benefits but are difficult to sustain long-term, both intermittent fasting and keto focus on the fundamentals of how you eat and the decisions you make at each meal. Intermittent fasting and keto are lifestyle modifications and long-term solutions for a healthier, happier you when done correctly.

Everything we want to know about anything is now at our fingertips, or only a swipe away, thanks to today's information availability. The same convenience may sometimes lead to an information overload. How can you go through it all and figure out whether keto and intermittent fasting are appropriate for you? That is the book's purpose. I dug deep into both lifestyles and evaluated the advantages of both practices—separately and in combination—so you can go to to the point and start your intermittent keto adventure.

Before you start making modifications, read the instructions from beginning to finish as you would any other recipe. Make sure you understand not just how to fast intermittently and prepare keto-friendly meals, but also the science behind it. The transition to this will be smoother if you read all of the introductory stuff.

Making the transition to a new lifestyle simpler and completing the 4-Week Plan. As tempting as it may be to go right to the 4-Week Plan and recipes, remember that success is built on a strong foundation. Between this introduction and the recipes, the words offer the foundation for a strong start.

Be ready for the sceptics. We'll go over this in more detail in the part below under "Before You Begin." Nowadays, everyone is an expert, willing to offer their thoughts whether they are accepted or not. Remember that you are the only one who knows all there is to know about yourself. You'll know whether intermittent keto is suitable for you after reading the next sections. Of course, if you have any underlying health problems, please seek medical advice before adopting any dietary or lifestyle changes.

WHAT EXACTLY IS KETOSIS?

Carbohydrates, on the surface, seem to be a convenient, frequently rapid, and low-cost source of energy. Consider all of the breakfast-related grab-and-go snacks: granola bars, fruit-filled smoothies, and muffins. We eat carbohydrates first thing in the morning and continue to do so throughout the day. Simply because something works does not imply that it is the most efficient method.

Our bodies' tissues and cells need energy to conduct daily tasks in order to keep us alive. The things we consume may provide them with energy from two different sources. Carbohydrates, which are converted to glucose, are one source of energy. That is the present model, which is followed by the majority of us. However, there is an alternative fuel, and it's a surprise one: fat. Yes, the exact thing you've been advised to avoid your whole life may be the key to kick-starting your metabolism. When our systems metabolise meals and break down fatty acids, organic molecules called ketones are produced. Ketones serve as a source of energy for our cells and muscles.

You've probably heard the term "metabolism" before, but do you really know what it means? The word simply refers to the chemical processes that all living organisms must do in order to remain alive. Given the complexity of the human body, our metabolism is everything from simple. Our bodies are always working. Our cells are constantly growing and mending themselves, even while we're asleep. They need to get energy from our bodies.

One method to fuel our metabolism is glucose, which is what carbohydrates are broken down into when we consume them. Carbohydrates are the main source of energy in our current nutritional recommendations. Take into account any extra sugars we consume, as well as the

There is no shortage of glucose in our systems if we eat the necessary daily amounts of fruit, starchy vegetables, grains, and plant-based sources of protein (e.g., beans). The issue with this energy consumption paradigm is that it makes us feel like hamsters on one of those wheels. We're eating more carbohydrates than our bodies can utilise in a day's work, so we're burning energy but going nowhere.

But there's also fat, which I stated before. So, how does it work? Is it conceivable that using that alternate fuel source can assist our bodies in burning energy more effectively, thus improving our general health? We're back to the old adage that you are what you eat, but this time think about the main principle while you burn your food. This is when ketosis enters the picture. Switching to a high-fat, moderate-protein, low-carb diet causes your body to enter a state of ketosis, in which fat is metabolised and ketones are released to power our intricate inner workings. After fatty acids are broken down, the liver produces ketones.

Balance is key to getting into ketosis, but not the type you're accustomed to when it comes to food. Our present food pyramid, which tells us to eat an excessive quantity of carbohydrate-rich meals for energy, is really backwards. Fats are at the top of the food pyramid, accounting for 60 to 80 percent of your diet; protein is in the centre, accounting for 20 to 30 percent; and carbohydrates (actually glucose disguised) are at the bottom, accounting for just 5 to 10% of your daily eating plan.

PALEO VS. KETO

Evolution provides us with many advantages. The capacity to cook with fire and electricity is evidence enough that development may be beneficial. A major gap occurred somewhere between our hunter-gatherer foraging lifestyle and today's contemporary civilization. Sure, we now live longer lives, but what about the quality of those additional years in terms of health? It's possible that the sluggish feeling you're experiencing isn't simply due to a lack of sleep (though sleep is usually beneficial!).

If food serves as fuel for our body, it's fair to assume that what we consume affects our productivity. When diesel is used in a vehicle that was intended to operate on gasoline, the results are catastrophic. Is it conceivable that our bodies are in a similar condition now as a consequence of our systems evolving to depend on carbohydrates for energy as food grew more reliable, rather than fat, as they were in our early days? I'm aware.

While this may seem eerily similar to pushing for a paleo diet, the ketogenic lifestyle's fundamental principles are radically different. Keto is all about establishing a harmony between what you eat and how your body works, which is why the emphasis is on macronutrient manipulation (fat, protein, carbohydrates, fiber, and fluids). Each calorie is made up of a combination of macronutrients. Understanding why you eat the way you do is crucial to understanding the larger picture.

Fiber, for example, helps food move through the digestive tract, keeping us regular. What goes in must come out, and fibre is necessary for this to happen. Protein assists in tissue healing, enzyme production, and the formation of bones, muscles, and skin. Fluids keep us hydrated; our cells, tissues, and organs can't operate correctly without them. Carbohydrates' main function is to produce energy, but in order to do so, the body must convert them into glucose, which has a cascading impact throughout the body. Because of its connection to insulin generation from increasing blood sugar levels, carb intake is a delicate balance for individuals with diabetes. Healthy fats assist to promote cell development, protect our organs, keep us warm, and give energy, but only when carbs are eaten in moderation. I'll explain why and how it occurs in a moment.

NET CARBS VS. CARBS

Carbohydrates may be found in virtually every dietary source in some way. Carbohydrate removal is both impossible and impractical. To operate, we need carbs. It's crucial to grasp this if we want to understand why certain limited meals on the keto diet are better options than others.

In the nutritional breakdown of a meal, fibre counts as a carb. It's crucial to note that fibre has no effect on our blood sugar levels, which is a good thing since fibre is a necessary macronutrient that aids in healthy digestion. Net carbohydrates are calculated by subtracting the quantity of fibre from the number of carbs in the nutritional tally of an item or completed dish.

Consider your salary before taxes (gross) and after taxes (net) (net). Perhaps a poor comparison, given that no one likes paying taxes, but one that is useful in attempting to comprehend carbohydrates vs. net carbs and how to monitor them. You consume a specific amount of carbohydrates, but not all of them have an effect on your blood sugar level.

This isn't to say you can't experiment with whole-grain pasta. Despite the fact that it's a healthier option than white-flour pasta, you should keep your net carbohydrates to 20 to 25 grammes per day. To put it in perspective, two ounces of uncooked whole-grain pasta has about 35 grammes of carbs and just 7 grammes of total fibre. People will most likely inquire about spaghetti and bread if you are missing them. The best way to respond is to share all you can eat (see the Keto

Cheat Sheet here).

HOW LONG DOES KETOSIS TAKE TO TAKE EFFECT?

Within one to three days, most individuals are in ketosis. Because everyone's body is different, it may take up to a week for some individuals. Your present body weight, nutrition, and amount of exercise are all factors that influence how fast you enter ketosis.

Your body must first burn up its glycogen (glucose) stores before entering ketosis. When your body's glycogen stores are exhausted, it's time to start breaking down those fatty acids. The liver receives the signal to start excreting ketones during the following several days. This last step signifies that you've reached ketosis. Because ketone levels will be relatively low unless you sustain ketosis for a long length of time, the early stage is moderate ketosis. Ketone levels may be officially measured (see here), but you may notice certain physiological changes that indicate ketosis, such as keto flu or keto breath. They aren't as severe or dramatic as they seem, and the advantages of ketosis may exceed the drawbacks during this phase-in stage as you work toward your objectives, but it's still a good idea to be aware of the symptoms (see here and here).

INTERMITTENT FASTING: WHAT DOES IT MEAN?

What is the first thing that comes to mind when you hear the phrase "Today I will fast?" I'm guessing it's "But I don't want to go hungry"? You're not alone in this common misunderstanding, so let's dissect it and make it more digestible (pun intended!).

Starvation vs. Fasting
Fasting is a deliberate decision. Fasting differs from hunger

in that it is a conscious choice to refrain from eating. You may pick how long you want to stay.

You are not obligated to fast or to fast for a specific reason (religious, weight loss, or detox). Fasting may be done at any time. Fasting, when done correctly, may be beneficial to our overall health.

Famine, poverty, and war are just a few reasons why people are forced to starve because of circumstances beyond their control. Starvation is a severe calorie deficit that may result in organ damage and death. No one chooses to go hungry.

It was lot simpler for me to get my mind around the notion of not eating once I thought about it from this viewpoint. Yes, I was first sceptical about fasting. My first reaction to the idea of not eating was always, "Why would anyone choose to starve?" before I realised there was a difference between fasting and starvation. The truth is that anyone who decides to fast is simply refusing to eat for a set period of time. Even peaceful protests that use fasting as a means of achieving a goal have a clear goal in mind.

Will You Be Hungry During Your Fast?

Let's start by putting the question in context. The truth is, we all fast once a day. We often eat our last meal a few hours before going to sleep, and except for nursing newborns, I can't think of anyone who eats the moment they wake. Even if you average only six hours of sleep a night, it's likely you're already fasting ten hours a day. Now let's add the idea of intermittent to the mix. "Intermittent" means something that is not continuous. When applying that to the idea of fasting, it means you're lengthening the time when you don't eat between meals (the word "breakfast" means just that, breaking the fast).

Since our bodies are already accustomed to fasting once a

day, the bigger issue is mind over matter. Let's get back to the question of whether you will feel hungry. The first week may be an adjustment as you get used to the extended period of time in your new fasting goal. To help you adjust, the 4-Week Intermittent Keto Plan here builds the fasting part of your day into your sleeping hours. It's quite possible your body will start to feel hungry around whatever time you're currently used to eating breakfast if it's before noon, but you will adjust within a few days.

In anticipation of the change you're about to make, try pushing back your first meal of the day by thirty minutes every day for a week before starting the 4- Week Plan. This way, when you begin the schedule laid out here, you'll need to

adjust your timing of your final meal of the day only once you begin week two of the plan for the Meals from Noon to 6 p.m. Only schedule.

Why Choose Intermittent Fasting?

Now that we've cleared up what it really means to fast, and you realise it's a conscious choice not to eat for a period of time, you might be still be wondering, why bother? The main reason that intermittent fasting (commonly referred to as IF) has taken the diet world by storm is its ability to promote weight loss. Metabolism is often categorised as one function of the human body. In reality, metabolism involves two essential reactions: catabolism and anabolism.

Catabolism is the part of metabolism wherein our bodies break down the food we consume. During catabolism, complex molecules are broken down into smaller units that release energy. Anabolism then uses that energy to begin the process of rebuilding and repairing our bodies, growing new cells, and maintaining tissues. Technically speaking, catabolism and anabolism happen simultaneously, but the rate at which they occur is different. A traditional eating schedule, where we spend the majority of our day eating, means our bodies have less time to spend in the second, or anabolic, phase of metabolism. It's a little confusing, perhaps, because the processes are interdependent, but remember that the rates at which they occur differ. The important takeaway here is that fasting for an elongated period allows for maximum efficiency in the metabolic processes.

Another amazing side effect of fasting, even for an intermittent period as outlined in this book, is a resurgence in mental acuity. Numerous studies show that contrary to popular belief, fasting makes you more aware and focused, not tired or light-headed. Many point to evolution and our ability to survive as a species: long before food preservation was possible, mental awareness was necessary at all times so that we could live from day to day, regardless of how plentiful food resources may have been.

Scientific research points toward neurogenesis, the growth and development of nerve tissue in the brain, kicking into high gear during periods of fasting.

All roads lead toward one exceptionally important conclusion when it comes to fasting: it allows your body time to do more of the behind-the-scenes work necessary. The longer you extend the window between eating your last meal of one day and consuming the first meal of the following one, the more time your body must focus on cellular regeneration and tissue repair at all levels.

Are Liquids Allowed When Fasting?

There's one last important detail to note about intermittent fasting. Unlike religious fasting, which generally restricts consuming any food or liquids during the fast period, IF allows you to consume certain liquids. Technically speaking, the moment you consume anything with calories, a fast is broken. Looking at it through the lens of using intermittent fasting for its weight-loss benefits means we can apply different rules.

Bone broth (here) is recommended to replenish vitamins and minerals, and to maintain sodium levels. Coffee and tea are allowed, preferably without any added milk or cream, and with absolutely no sweeteners. There are two schools of thought on adding dairy to your coffee or tea. Provided it's only a high-fat addition, such as coconut oil or butter to make bulletproof coffee (here), many keto advocates think it's fine, since it doesn't disrupt ketosis. Adding MCT (medium-chain triglyceride) oil is believed to boost energy levels and leave you feeling sated as well. Purists adhere to plain coffee or tea. You should do what works best for you, provided it doesn't kick you out of ketosis (for ways to test for this, see here) (for ways to test for this, see here).

Let's not forget water, as staying well hydrated is essential to any healthy lifestyle choices. Caffeine can be especially depleting, so make sure to balance coffee consumption with water intake too.

THE POWER OF INTERMITTENT FASTING & KETO COMBINED

By now, the benefits of intermittent fasting and adhering to a keto diet should be evident. What you might not have pieced together is the connection between the two. When you're in ketosis, that process of breaking down fatty acids to produce ketones for fuel is actually what the body does to keep itself going when you're fasting. What does it mean to combine the two, and why bother blending these lifestyles and ways of eating?

Fasting for one to two days has a significant effect when eating a traditional carb-centric diet. After the initial phase of burning glucose (that is, carbohydrates) for energy, your body naturally switches to burning fat as fuel.

You see where I'm going here, right? If it takes twenty-four to forty-eight hours for your body to switch to burning fat for fuel, imagine the effects of combining intermittent fasting with keto. Maintaining a constant state of ketosis means your body is already burning fat for fuel. This means the longer you

spend in a state of fasting, the longer you're burning fat. Intermittent fasting combined with keto makes fasting's weight-loss effects more efficient, often resulting in more weight loss than traditional diets. The prolonged time between your last and first meals of the day means extra fat-burning capabilities for your body.

Ketosis is often used in body building because it's a safe way to shed fat without losing muscle. Weight loss is good only when it's the right weight, and we all need muscle mass to stay healthy.

How Does It Work?

Switching to the keto diet is a huge lifestyle change. For that reason, it's best to ease into the intermittent fasting aspect of this programme. Let your body adjust to a new way of eating, get adapted to burning fat for fuel, and deal with any possible side effects (remember keto flu is a possibility) before incorporating intermittent fasting into your eating routine, or in this case, your extended period of not eating. Notice that intermittent fasting is not introduced until Week 2 of the 4-Week Plan.

During the phase-in period, you'll want to take note of eating times. Even before you incorporate the intermittent-fasting component of the plan, your last meal of the day should be no later than 6 p.m. This will ease you into fasting and help you avoid snacking. One of the effects of keto is that it trains your body— and, let's face it, your brain—to eat only when you're hungry. As times goes by, cravings cease. We often confuse cravings with hunger, when really cravings are a learned behaviour, whereas hunger is a physiological call to refuel our energy reserves.

Timing Your Fasting Period

How you decide to incorporate your intermittent-fasting time is a bit flexible. Do you tend to dive into the water head first, or do you dip your toes in first? Knowing that about your personality will help you determine which schedule is better for you. In talking with my editor while writing this book, I learned that what was appealing to me was not to her.

I don't like feeling in a rut, and breakfast is one of my favourite meals of the day, so for me, having an alternate schedule that allows me to eat breakfast and abstain from dinner just about every other day, and to do the reverse on the other

days (fasting through breakfast and eating dinner), is preferable. My editor, Marisa, prefers consistency, something I imagine a lot of people might want as well—to go on auto-pilot and fast at the same time every day. I can see how one or the other would fit into certain lifestyles and mind-sets, and that's why there are two schedules to choose from (here) (here). They allow you to customise the Intermittent Keto Plan to fit best with your lifestyle.

BEFORE YOU GET STARTED

Looking at the big picture is key to long-term success in any situation. This holds especially true for major diet and lifestyle changes. Intermittent keto throws everything you thought you knew about how to eat, what to eat, and when to eat it out the window. It's not a leap-without-looking kind of decision, so it's important to familiarise yourself with what to expect, how to handle potential challenges, and how to reorganise your life in a way that enables you to achieve your goals before starting out.

Define Your Goals

Why did you decide to try intermittent keto? Is it for health reasons? Weight loss? Are you looking just to feel better and increase your energy levels? Is this meant to be a short-term detox or are you looking to make long-term lifestyle changes? How do you plan to keep track of your macronutrients? Do you plan to test for ketones to ensure you've reached a state of ketosis? Are you vegetarian or vegan?

All are important questions to consider before getting started so you can stay focused on achieving your goal. Research suggests that intermittent fasting can have profound long-term benefits. The verdict is still out on the benefits or any potential risks of implementing a keto diet permanently. The rigidity of the plan also dictates the length of time people adhere to it.

The way you currently eat is also a big consideration when you undertake keto, and you should understand how big a change or challenge that might pose. Keto is a fat-focused diet macronutrient-wise, but protein plays an important role. Too little protein can cause muscle loss during ketosis. Too much can kick you out of ketosis. It's a balance, and while keto is not a high-protein diet, the default protein is often meat because the plant-based protein alternatives typically touted are too high in carbs compared with their ratio of fibre and

protein, specifically beans, including tofu (which is made from soybeans) (which is made from soybeans).

This doesn't mean it's impossible to stay vegetarian on keto, especially if you're an ovo-lacto vegetarian (okay with eating eggs and dairy) (okay with eating eggs and dairy). Nonmeat protein sources that are not legumes include eggs, nuts and seeds, and cheese. The recipes in this book are geared toward an omnivorous diet. Meat plays a role in many of the recipes. You'll need to customise your meal plan, supplementing it with recipes from outside sources. The rest of the information included in this book will be extremely helpful, and this applies to vegans, too. If you want to give intermittent keto a try with a vegan diet, it is not impossible, but it will require even more careful planning to make sure you don't kick yourself out of ketosis by choosing protein sources too high in carbs. Many of the recipes in this book will need adjusting for your dietary needs, as well.

Testing for ketosis can be done in three ways: urine test strips; a blood ketone test (with a metre similar to the kind used to test blood-glucose levels); and a breath test (different from keto breath, which is discussed separately) (different from keto breath, which is discussed separately). Urine tests are considered the least effective, but they are the least expensive, with blood metres considered the most accurate. They are also, as you might've guessed, the costliest.

The fundamental issue is whether or not you should test for ketones. After the first few weeks, if your objective is to lose weight and the pounds are falling off while you feel well (well rested and energetic), testing for ketosis may be a moot issue. When it comes to counting numbers, the most essential aspect is keeping track of what you're consuming.

Which Should You Count: Macronutrients or Calories?
Counting calories is not the same as tracking macronutrients. The focus keto is on keeping track of how much fat, protein, and carbs you consume—each macronutrient has its own calorie count:

9 calories per gramme of fat
4 calories per gramme of protein
4 calories per gramme of carbohydrate

Counting macronutrients seems to be more difficult than it is. It's really simply a matter of paying closer attention to each calorie eaten. It's still essential to establish a metabolic baseline.

BMR, or basal metabolic rate, is used to calculate how many calories you should consume for weight maintenance and weight reduction (another reason why defining your goals is important).
All of these macronutrients are important for your general health as well as getting into and remaining in ketosis, but carbs are the one that receive the most attention on keto since they produce glucose during metabolism which is the energy source you're trying to avoid. According to some studies, the real number of total carbohydrates one may eat per day on keto is 50 grammes or less—resulting in 20 to 35 net carbs per day, depending on the fibre level. The less net carbohydrates you consume, the quicker your body will enter ketosis and the simpler it will be to remain there.
Keeping in mind that we want to eat 20 grammes of net carbohydrates per day, the fat and protein grammes will vary depending on how many calories you need to take based on your BMR. For weight management, women should consume between 1,600 and 2,000 calories per day, depending on their level of exercise (from sedentary to active). Following

a daily diet of 160 grammes of fat, 70 grammes of protein, and 20 grammes of carbs corresponds to 1,800 calories of eating, which is the USDA's recommended amount for weight maintenance in moderately active women (walking 1.5 to 3 miles a day). If you live a sedentary lifestyle, you should aim for 130 grammes of fat, 60 grammes of protein, and 20 grammes of carbs to help you lose weight (1500 calories). There are several online calculators available to help you calculate your BMR and total calorie target, as well as the proper fat and protein ratio while keeping net carbohydrates under 20 grammes per day.

In the spirit of calculators and numbers, you may find it useful to create a macronutrient tracking system using the recipes in this book to help design your own unique meal. It's as simple as jotting it down in a notepad and performing the arithmetic, but that might take a long time. There are many of applications for your phone that make monitoring macronutrients simple.

THE PHYSICAL CONSEQUENCES OF THE KETO DIET
Unlike other weight-loss diets that merely restrict what you consume, keto goes a step farther. Ketosis entails altering your eating habits in order to alter the way your body turns food into energy. The ketosis process changes the equation.

Using fat instead of glucose (remember, carbohydrates) as a source of energy. As your body adapts to a new method of operating, you may experience adverse effects. This is also why the 4-Week Plan introduces intermittent fasting in week two rather than right away. It's critical to allow oneself enough time to adapt, both physically and psychologically. Keto fever and keto breath are two bodily changes that you may encounter while starting a keto diet.

Keto Flu is a term used to describe a condition
Keto flu, often known as carb flu, may range from a few days to many weeks. Increased sensations of tiredness, irritability, muscular pain, light-headedness or brain fog, change in bowel motions, nausea, stomachaches, and difficulty focusing and concentrating may occur when your body

weans itself off using glucose for energy. I know, it sounds awful, and i probably something you've heard before. Yes, they are all typical flu symptoms, thus the name.

The good news is that this is just a phase that your body will go through while it adapts, and it does not impact everyone. Electrolyte imbalances (sodium, potassium, magnesium, and calcium) and sugar withdrawal fro substantially reduced carbohydrate intake are among the causes of these symptoms. If you anticipate these symptoms, you'll be better prepared to relieve them and shorten the duration of the keto flu, if it occurs.

The quantity of highly processed foods you eat has a direct impact on your sodium levels. To be clear, everything we eat is technically a processed food; the phrase "processed food" refers to "a sequence of procedures used to accomplish a certain goal." Even cooking from scrat at home requires food processing. However, in our contemporary societ when ready-to-eat meals can be found at every corner of the store, these highly processed foods are more likely to have excessive amounts of concealed salt (sodium is a preservative as well as a flavour enhancer). When you're doing the cooking, you can manage the quantity of carbohydrates and sugars in a meal, making it easier to stick to a keto di Home cooking is less processed, which may result in lower sodium leve Increasing the salt in your meals and drinking a homemade stock like th bone broth below are two simple, natural methods to increase your sodium levels.

Other foods to concentrate on throughout your keto phase-in period are listed below. They're high in magnesium, potassium, and calcium, which may help keep your bones strong.

equilibrium of electrolytes

Magnesium is a mineral found in the human body (helps with muscle soreness and leg cramps)
Avocados, broccoli, seafood, kale, almonds, pumpkin seeds, and spinacl are some of the healthy foods you may eat. Potassium is a mineral found in many foods (helps with muscle soreness, hydration)
Asparagus, avocados, Brussels sprouts, salmon, tomatoes, and leafy

greens are just a few of the ingredients. Calcium is a mineral that is found in (especially important if you were a big milk drinker pre-keto) Almonds, bok choy, broccoli, cheddar, collard greens, spinach, sardines, sesame seeds, and chia seeds are just a few of the ingredients.

Another approach to reduce your chances of getting keto flu is to start reducing your carb consumption gradually a few weeks before beginning the 4-Week Plan. It may be as easy as substituting a hard-boiled or scrambled egg for your morning muffin, foregoing the bread and wrapping your burger in lettuce (commonly referred to as protein-style when ordering), or substituting spaghetti for zoodles. When you start the plan here or here, it will seem more like a gradual progression toward eating less carbohydrates rather than a drastic change in your diet. The fundamental issue is whether or not you should test for ketones. After the first few weeks, if your objective is to lose weight and the pounds are falling off while you feel well (well rested and energetic), testing for ketosis may be a moot issue. When it comes to counting numbers, the most essential aspect is keeping track of what you're consuming.

Which Should You Count: Macronutrients or Calories?
Counting calories is not the same as tracking macronutrients. The focus of keto is on keeping track of how much fat, protein, and carbs you consume—each macronutrient has its own calorie count:

9 calories per gramme of fat
4 calories per gramme of protein
4 calories per gramme of carbohydrate

Counting macronutrients seems to be more difficult than it is. It's really simply a matter of paying closer attention to each calorie eaten. It's still essential to establish a metabolic baseline.

BMR, or basal metabolic rate, is used to calculate how many calories you should consume for weight maintenance and weight reduction (another reason why defining your goals is important).

All of these macronutrients are important for your general health as wel
as getting into and remaining in ketosis, but carbs are the one that recei
the most attention on keto since they produce glucose during metabolis
which is the energy source you're trying to avoid. According to some
studies, the real number of total carbohydrates one may eat per day on
keto is 50 grammes or less—resulting in 20 to 35 net carbs per day,
depending on the fibre level. The less net carbohydrates you consume, t
quicker your body will enter ketosis and the simpler it will be to remain
there.

Keeping in mind that we want to eat 20 grammes of net carbohydrates p
day, the fat and protein grammes will vary depending on how many
calories you need to take based on your BMR. For weight management
women should consume between 1,600 and 2,000 calories per day,
depending on their level of exercise (from sedentary to active). Followi
a daily diet of 160 grammes of fat, 70 grammes of protein, and 20
grammes of carbs corresponds to 1,800 calories of eating, which is the
USDA's recommended amount for weight maintenance in moderately
active women (walking 1.5 to 3 miles a day). If you live a sedentary
lifestyle, you should aim for 130 grammes of fat, 60 grammes of protei
and 20 grammes of carbs to help you lose weight (1500 calories). There
are several online calculators available to help you calculate your BMR
and total calorie target, as well as the proper fat and protein ratio while
keeping net carbohydrates under 20 grammes per day.

In the spirit of calculators and numbers, you may find it useful to create
macronutrient tracking system using the recipes in this book to help
design your own unique meal. It's as simple as jotting it down in a
notepad and performing the arithmetic, but that might take a long time.
There are many of applications for your phone that make monitoring
macronutrients simple.

THE PHYSICAL CONSEQUENCES OF THE KETO DIET
Unlike other weight-loss diets that merely restrict what you consume,
keto goes a step farther. Ketosis entails altering your eating habits in or
to alter the way your body turns food into energy. The ketosis process
changes the equation.

Using fat instead of glucose (remember, carbohydrates) as a source of energy. As your body adapts to a new method of operating, you may experience adverse effects. This is also why the 4-Week Plan introduces intermittent fasting in week two rather than right away. It's critical to allow oneself enough time to adapt, both physically and psychologically. Keto fever and keto breath are two bodily changes that you may encounter while starting a keto diet.

Keto Flu is a term used to describe a condition
Keto flu, often known as carb flu, may range from a few days to many weeks. Increased sensations of tiredness, irritability, muscular pain, light-headedness or brain fog, change in bowel motions, nausea, stomachaches, and difficulty focusing and concentrating may occur when your body weans itself off using glucose for energy. I know, it sounds awful, and it's probably something you've heard before. Yes, they are all typical flu symptoms, thus the name.
The good news is that this is just a phase that your body will go through while it adapts, and it does not impact everyone. Electrolyte imbalances (sodium, potassium, magnesium, and calcium) and sugar withdrawal from substantially reduced carbohydrate intake are among the causes of these symptoms. If you anticipate these symptoms, you'll be better prepared to relieve them and shorten the duration of the keto flu, if it occurs.
The quantity of highly processed foods you eat has a direct impact on your sodium levels. To be clear, everything we eat is technically a processed food; the phrase "processed food" refers to "a sequence of procedures used to accomplish a certain goal." Even cooking from scratch at home requires food processing. However, in our contemporary society, when ready-to-eat meals can be found at every corner of the store, these highly processed foods are more likely to have excessive amounts of concealed salt (sodium is a preservative as well as a flavour enhancer). When you're doing the cooking, you can manage the quantity of carbohydrates and sugars in a meal, making it easier to stick to a keto diet. Home cooking is less processed, which may result in lower sodium levels. Increasing the salt in your meals and drinking a homemade stock like the

bone broth below are two simple, natural methods to increase your sodium levels.

Other foods to concentrate on throughout your keto phase-in period are listed below. They're high in magnesium, potassium, and calcium, whic may help keep your bones strong.

equilibrium of electrolytes

Magnesium is a mineral found in the human body (helps with muscle soreness and leg cramps)
Avocados, broccoli, seafood, kale, almonds, pumpkin seeds, and spinac are some of the healthy foods you may eat. Potassium is a mineral foun in many foods (helps with muscle soreness, hydration)
Asparagus, avocados, Brussels sprouts, salmon, tomatoes, and leafy greens are just a few of the ingredients. Calcium is a mineral that is fou in (especially important if you were a big milk drinker pre-keto)
Almonds, bok choy, broccoli, cheddar, collard greens, spinach, sardines sesame seeds, and chia seeds are just a few of the ingredients.

Another approach to reduce your chances of getting keto flu is to start reducing your carb consumption gradually a few weeks before beginnin the 4-Week Plan. It may be as easy as substituting a hard-boiled or scrambled egg for your morning muffin, foregoing the bread and wrapping your burger in lettuce (commonly referred to as protein-style when ordering), or substituting spaghetti for zoodles. When you start th plan here or here, it will seem more like a gradual progression toward eating less carbohydrates rather than a drastic change in your diet.

Keto Breath

Let's go right to the point. Bad breath sucks, to put it bluntly, but that's something you should expect while going keto. There are two possible explanations for why this happens.

Acetone is one of the ketones produced when your body enters ketosis and starts producing ketones (a by-product of burning fat for fuel) (yes, the same solvent found in nail polish remover and paint thinners). In an effort to complete the metabolic process of breaking down those fatty acids, acetone is expelled via urine and breath. This may lead to breath that smells bad.

Protein may also have a role in causing keto breath. Remember that the macronutrient aim is to have a high fat, moderate protein, and low carbohydrate diet. Many people mistakenly believe that high fat and high protein are synonymous. That is not the case. Fat and protein are digested in various ways by the body. When our systems break down protein, they create ammonia, which they typically expel via urine. When you eat more protein than you need, the indigestible portion remains in your intestines.

It ferments in your digestive tract, generating ammonia, which is subsequently exhaled.

On the plus side, keto breath is a reliable indication that your body is in ketosis. The length of time the scent lasts depends on how effectively your body adjusts to ketosis. According to several reports, it may last anywhere from a week to slightly under a month. A closer look into keto message boards and chat groups reveals that it may last for months, while some claim to have never experienced it. Always have sugar-free gum on hand, reduce your protein intake, maintain a good dental routine (brushing and flossing), and follow the advice mentioned earlier on gradually reducing your carbohydrate intake before jumping full steam ahead into the 4-Week Plan are some solutions to possibly avoid or lessen keto breath.

EXERCISE AND SLEEP

A healthy lifestyle involves getting enough sleep and engaging in moderate physical exercise. When it comes to establishing your objectives and working out how they fit into your everyday routine, the same guidance applies. Because those sleeping hours are part of your fasting period when you include intermittent fasting into your schedule, they become even more important. Tucking down at a decent hour will keep late-night munching cravings at bay.

Weight training is popular among keto dieters, and it's especially essential when you're on a maintenance diet. Cardio exercises are the most effective fat-burning activities when it comes to weight reduction. If you have any underlying health problems, talk to your doctor before making any significant adjustments.

CONSULT YOUR FRIENDS AND FAMILY.

When the term "diet" is spoken, most individuals have strong feelings about it, which become even stronger when specific diet programmes are mentioned. Everyone has the right to their own views, and discussing comparable experiences may be beneficial when seeking inspiration or motivation. People who say things like "You look great the way you are" or "I could never give up carbohydrates" or, even worse, "You're going to starve yourself?" are not helpful.

Consider yourself the helmsman of your body, as every ship requires a helmsman. Friends and family should be there to support you on your journey, so provide them with the necessary information. Tell them why you're making the decision you're making.

If you're comfortable talking about it, the switch. At the very least, explain why intermittent fasting and keto diets work so effectively for certain individuals. People are often perplexed by what they don't understand, and they don't take the time to learn more. If they wish to learn more about the diet, you may even gift them a copy of this book. You never know whether you'll encourage someone else to try intermittent keto as well, and then you'll have someone to keep track of your success, establish goals with, and keep you inspired.

Sharing your keto choice is also a smart way to prevent coming up to a friend's dinner party and finding out they're just offering spaghetti. In such a situation, you should offer to bring a dish to share that is also keto-friendly so that you can enjoy it. This way, your host won't be as stressed about preparing for you, and you'll be able to sample some of the delicious keto dishes!

There will be some who believe they know better or who believe it is OK to cheat occasionally. That may be true for other diets, but eating too many carbs may quickly push you out of ketosis. Be your own best advocate, and don't be scared to say no thank you. People who care about you will not attempt to entice you since you are working hard to create a better lifestyle for yourself.

When making arrangements, you should obviously keep your intermittent fasting regimen in mind. Late-night meals aren't really in the cards, but you may meet for drinks and have simple seltzer with a lime wedge, or better yet, meet for coffee after dinner. The 4-Week Plan was created to offer you a respite from intermittent fasting on Sunday mornings, bearing in mind that brunch is a popular time to get together with friends and is extremely simple to follow on the keto diet.

HOW TO KEEP IN KETOSIS AND WHAT TO DO IF YOU FALL OUT

After you've completed the 4-Week Plan, you may select how long you want to stay in ketosis. Was it just a matter of dropping a dress size for you? It's possible that a month will suffice. Were you attempting to wean yourself off sugar or cut down on your carb consumption in general? Even if you opt to raise your total carb intake above the 20 grammes per day allowed in the 4-Week Plan, a little longer may be beneficial to help you develop long-term eating habits. Anything fewer than 50 grammes of carbs (total, not net carbs) helps your body enter fat-burning mode, so even a little increase in carbs may put you in a moderate state of ketosis.

Despite the fact that you may regain some of the weight you lost at first, you will reap the benefits.

Prepare yourself for steep learning curves and potential hazards. If you consume too much protein, too many carbohydrates, or don't get enough exercise, you may knock your body out of ketosis. A simple blunder, or just giving in to a desire, like eating a sweet potato, may send your body back into glucose-burning mode.

If keto seems to be rigorous, it's because it is. Getting into ketosis and staying there takes dedication, which is why we spoke about setting objectives early on. Don't be too harsh on yourself if it seems catastrophic or disappointing after all your hard effort. Concentrate on your long-term objectives and getting back into ketosis. Don't keep cheating because you think, "Oh, well, the harm is done." Instead, fasting after a cheat day may help you get back on track, but bear in mind that you'll need to burn off the glucose again first.

Journaling is a wonderful method to monitor more than just calories in general. Start keeping track of how you're feeling physically and mentally—a basic numerical grading system may help you figure out if you're making progress, maintaining the status quo, or falling behind on your objectives. Detailed notes may help you identify more clear causes for your cheat day in the future, allowing you to prepare better. In fact, you may want to build in cheat days so you can anticipate them rather than punishing yourself for having them. Plan ahead if you know your closest friend's wedding is approaching and you'll want to participate in all of the festivities, including all of the food and drink provided. While you won't be able to just switch back into ketosis, you'll know what to anticipate and be able to get back on track faster than before. It's also worth noting that you shouldn't depend on cheat days too often. This goes back to establishing your objectives.

KNOW WHAT FOODS TO ENJOY & WHAT FOODS TO AVOID

It's all too tempting to concentrate on what you can't eat on keto, but it's far more enjoyable to think about all the things you can. When you're in need of some motivation, look to the chart below.

CHEAT SHEET FOR THE KETO DIET

Zoodles, spaghetti squash, and shirataki noodles are all good options.

Pasta should be avoided.

Eat: Use almond flour, unsweetened coconut flakes and pork cracklings

Bread crumbs should be avoided.

Cauliflower rice and shirataki rice are two dishes to try.

Rice and couscous should be avoided.

Heavy cream and cheeses are good to eat (mozzarella, cheddar)

Milk should be avoided.

Eat: Low-carb tortillas and keto bread (here) (here)

Bread, wraps, and tortillas should all be avoided.

Cauliflower purée is a delicious way to start the day.
Mashed potatoes should be avoided.

Eat: Zucchini fries
Avoid: French fries and sweet potato fries

Eat: Berries; add lemons and limes for taste
Avoid: Sweet citrus (oranges, grapefruit, clementines),
tropical fruits (bananas, mango, pineapple), all dried fruits

Eat: Meat, poultry, fish, eggs
Avoid: Beans, tofu

Eat: Stevia, monk fruit
Avoid: Sweeteners (honey, maple syrup, sugar) (honey,
maple syrup, sugar)

Eat: Olive oil, coconut oil, avocado oil, butter, ghee, sesame
oil (in tiny amounts) (in small quantities)
Avoid: Sunflower, grapeseed, canola, peanut, safflower oils,
margarine, vegetable shortening

Eat: Parmesan Crisps (here) (here)
Avoid: Chips and sweet/salty snacks

Eat: Water (key for staying hydrated), coffee, tea
Avoid: Sugary drinks (soda, juices), alcohol

The Keto Kitchen
Leading up to starting intermittent keto, it's important to
make sure your pantry aligns with your new eating goals.

Those new goals might also be at odds with the rest of the members in your household, be they family or roommates. If so, clearing out all the carb-laden foods, sugary snacks, and processed foods might not be a possibility. In that case, it'll be an exercise in self-control for you, especially during the first week or two, when cravings might be tricky to manage. Don't fret. You can still claim an area of the kitchen and set up a keto- friendly zone to make sticking to the plan easier. And by all means, if you live on your own, or if your partner/family is doing this with you, go full throttle and use an out-with-the-old, in-with-the-new approach. Instead of discarding unwanted items, donate them to a local food pantry (check expiration dates first), or give them to your neighbours.

Once you've got a clean slate, it's time to start filling the pantry with all the foods you can enjoy. Here are staple ingredients you'll want to add to your first shopping list.

Fermented foods (make sure veggies are lacto-fermented): pickles, kimchi, sauerkraut, plain full-fat yoghurt

Oils: avocado oil, extra virgin olive oil, cold-pressed or virgin coconut oil, ghee, MCT oil

Nuts and seeds (and flours made from them): almonds, walnuts, macadamia nuts, brazil nuts, pecans, chia seeds, pumpkin seeds, sunflower seeds, sesame seeds, almond flour or meal, coconut flour

Canned goods and other shelf-stable items (make sure all nut milks are unsweetened): coconut cream, coconut milk, almond milk, olives, dark chocolate (Lily's dark chocolate chips are sweetened with stevia), cocoa powder, tea and coffee (plain, unflavored), pork rinds, baking powder (see note below) (see note below)

Spices and sweeteners: red pepper flakes, basil, oregano, bay leaves, smoked paprika, sea salts, black pepper, cumin, curry powder, everything- bagel seasoning, whole-grain mustard, stevia, monk fruit sweetener (read the label to make sure it's not a blend mixed with sugar)

Perishables: bacon and sausage (be sure to buy sugar-free varieties), eggs, coconut wraps, low-carb tortillas, sugar-free mayonnaise, heavy cream,

butter, cheese

A Word About Baking Powder & Other Ingredients

One look at the ingredients and you'll notice there's cornstarch in commercial baking powder. It's actually in most homemade recipes, too. Baking powder is traditionally made with a combination of baking soda, cream of tartar, and cornstarch. Some keto folks will tell you cornstarch is absolutely forbidden, since it's a grain and you're not supposed to eat any grains on keto. It's important to remember why you're not supposed to eat grains, though, before settling on a conclusion about baking powder. The underlying reason is that grains are carb heavy, and keto is a low-carb diet. The reality is, the amount of cornstarch in baking powder compared with how much you actually use in a recipe is so negligible that it barely registers. If you're grain free for health reasons, that's a good reason to make your own baking powder or seek out a brand without any cornstarch. I've yet to find one that exists, but that may change by the printing of this book. All the recipes in this book were tested using store-bought baking powder. Results using a homemade version without cornstarch aren't guaranteed.

Most bacon has sugar added during the curing process, even bacon from small, artisanal farmers. While the actual amount of sugar in the end product is minimal, you might want to look for a brand that has no sugar added if you're having trouble balancing your carb count.

Not all ketchups are created equal. In fact, many are loaded with sugar. Be sure to buy an unsweetened brand like Primal Kitchen for dipping and to make the BBQ sauce here.

Many keto enthusiasts swear by MCT oil. It's not coconut oil, but rather a by-product of coconut. MCT stands for medium chain triglycerides. Among the health benefits it is said to offer are that it keeps you satiated (feeling full), provides a quick boost of energy, and supports a healthy immune system. The full feeling it offers may be why some people believe it aids in weight loss, in that it prevents you from overeating or snacking.

Weekly Grocery Shopping
When it comes to produce, all herbs get a green light—great news, since they're easy flavour boosters to any meal. The general rule of thumb for vegetables is that

you should stick to ones that grow aboveground. That means steer clear of root vegetables and tubers (think carrots, parsnips, beets, onions, and regular and sweet potatoes), as they're starchier vegetables, higher in carbohydrates. Some aboveground vegetables are high-carb, too, such as winter squash, pumpkin, corn, and peas.
You can still eat the rainbow, so don't worry—dark, leafy greens (kale, spinach), broccoli, cauliflower, zucchini (zoodles!), radishes, cucumbers, garlic, asparagus, mushrooms, and eggplant all make the list for keto meals.
Fruit lovers might find keto challenging, since most fruits are too high in natural sugars and therefore off-limits, especially dried fruits—which have higher concentrations of sugar. Your choices are basically berries (since they're mostly fibre),

lemon, and limes. All other citrus fruits are too high in natural sugars. But guess what? If you love an orange essence in some dishes, you can use orange zest to add flavour without getting any of the carbs!

At this point, you might feel weighed down by all the things you can't eat. That's a normal feeling, and while it's a reality if you're committed to keto, I always prefer to focus on the foods you can eat, so snap a photo of that Keto Cheat Sheet here, and you'll always have a quick reference point when in doubt.

Essential Kitchen Tools

Veteran cooks likely have a well-stocked kitchen. If you're just starting out, you'll quickly realise that cooking your own food increases your success in sticking to a keto diet. I tend to stay away from gadgets that serve only one purpose, but exceptions to that rule are my spiralizer and avocado slicer. Homemade zoodles are a breeze to make with my handheld spiralizer, found in the hardware store's kitchen section for less than $20.

Avocados are a keto fan-favorite. Pitting avocados also results in more emergency-room visits than you might imagine and can even result in nerve damage. This happened to a dear friend of mine who's an experienced cook. She now owns an avocado slicer.

Regarding skillets, I find nonstick to be great if you can buy only one set of pans. Even though you'll be consuming considerably more fat than you do in your current diet, nonstick skillets are great for making eggs and pancakes (check out the Blueberry Almond Pancakes here) (check out the Blueberry Almond Pancakes here).

Here's a list of kitchen tools and equipment that you'll find helpful in preparing meals:

8-inch skillet 10-inch skillet Spiralizer

Digital kitchen scale

Bento box for packing lunches Tongs and spatula

Avocado slicer

Mason jars (for preparing and transporting chia puddings) (for preparing and transporting chia puddings) Silicon candy moulds (for making fat bombs) (for making fat bombs)

Chef's knife and paring knife

Variety of saucepans (ranging from 2 quarts to 8 quarts, if space and budget permit) (ranging from 2 quarts to 8 quarts, if space and budget permit)

Cutting boards Blender

Food processor (optional, but especially helpful to grind your own nut flours) (optional, but especially helpful to grind your own nut flours)

WHEN TO STOP & HOW TO STOP

Keto is strict about what you can and cannot eat. Throw in intermittent fasting and you further restrict when you can eat. Before you dive into your 4-Week Plan, this is a good time to talk about how long you should stay on keto and continue your intermittent fasting. Currently there isn't enough research to make a conclusion from a health perspective as to keto's long-term efficacy, but the truth is you're fighting your body's natural instinct to fuel itself on glucose. Even though we evolved under the premise of fat for fuel, times have changed, and along with that, so have our bodies—for better or for worse.

Although research providing concrete theories of how the keto diet works (besides those related to underlying medical issues) is lacking, many people lean toward using keto a few times a year for a prolonged period of time—anywhere from a few weeks to a couple of months—taking a break in between but still being mindful of overall carb consumption.

Intermittent fasting is a different storey. I know someone who's been fasting intermittently for a few years now. Her approach is different from the plan

outlined here, and she is not on keto, so her experience is different, but intermittent fasting has been very successful and manageable for her to maintain. She's also one of the biggest foodies and cooks I know, and intermittent fasting hasn't cramped her style one bit. Quite the opposite, in fact. She looks forward to her fast days, as they leave her feeling refreshed and focused. Should you decide to step away from the keto diet and stay with intermittent fasting, I suggest doing some research to figure out the best method and schedule for yourself.

When you feel you've reached the end of your keto journey or just want to press pause for a duration beyond a cheat, you must do it in a meaningful and methodical way. Remember that it took time for your body to adjust to ketosis. The same goes for reverting to a diet that has more carbohydrates, which will flip the switch back to burning glucose for energy. This applies even if your plan is to stay on a lower-carb diet than you ate before starting keto.

Things to keep in mind when you decide to switch off keto are:

Take it slowly, introducing more carbs a little at a time. Expect some weight gain. The amount depends on how long you've been on keto. The early weeks of weight loss on keto tend to be water weight. If you've been on keto for a while, the weight gain should be less, provided you're not overindulging in carbs and sugar.

Familiarize yourself with healthy portion sizes again, adjusting the quality of fats and proteins accordingly.

PART II
MEAL PLANS AND RECIPES

READY, SET, GO: 4-WEEK PLANS &RECIPES

MEAL PLANS

The Weekend Before\sSaturday. Clean out the pantry. Make shopping lists.
Sunday. Go grocery shopping—stick to the perimeter; all the super-processed items tend to be clustered in the middle aisles. Prep food for the week ahead.

4-WEEK PLAN—MEALS FROM NOON TO 6 P.M. ONLY
This plan allows for one day a week without fasting. It anticipates that you might want to enjoy a Sunday brunch with friends (keto foods only) (keto foods only). If you want, you can omit breakfast to stick with your IF routine. Just be sure to include a midday snack to make sure you consume your necessary macronutrients.

RECIPES\sCookbooks are generally broken into traditional categories
breakfast, lunch, dinner, and sweets and snacks. You'll find the recipes
up that way for familiarity. Since keto is all about focusing on y
macronutrients, what really matters is eating the right ratios of fat, prote
and carbs. Keeping that in mind, feel free to swap out breakfast for lun
lunch for dinner, or even dinner for

breakfast. Just track your macros to make sure you don't overeat any
them.

BREAKFAST

Pecan & Coconut 'n' Oatmeal Bacon, Egg & Cheese Breakfast "Muffin
Cheddar Chive Baked Avocado Eggs Blueberry Almond Pancakes
Toad in a Hole Berry Breakfast Shake\sCheddar, Spinach & Mushro
Omelet

PECAN & COCONUT 'N' OATMEAL \sServes: 1

This is a hearty breakfast porridge for cold mornings when you're craving a steaming bowl of oatmeal but don't want the carb overload.

½ cup coconut or almond milk 2 teaspoons chia seeds 2 tablespoons almond flour 1 tablespoon flax meal
tablespoons hemp hearts ¼ teaspoon ground cinnamon ¼ teaspoon pure vanilla extract 1 tablespoon pecans, toasted and chopped 1 tablespoon coconut flakes
In a small pot, combine the milk, chia seeds, almond flour, flax meal, hemp hearts, cinnamon, and vanilla. Cook over low heat, stirring constantly until thickened, about 5 minutes. Spoon into a bowl, top with the pecans and coconut flakes, and enjoy immediately.

Calories 312 Fat 25 Protein 13.4 Carbs 7 Fiber 5 Net carbs 2

BACON, EGG & CHEESE BREAKFAST "MUFFINS"
Makes: 6

6 slices bacon 8 eggs ¼ cup heavy cream Fine sea salt and freshly ground black pepper to taste 3 ounces shredded cheddar cheese
Preheat the oven to 375°F. Generously grease the bottoms and sides of a 6-cup muffin tin (softened butter works best for this) (softened butter works best for this).
Add the bacon to a cold 10-inch skillet, and place over medium-high heat. Cook until crisp all over, turning once. Transfer to a paper-towel line plate. Crumble the bacon into pieces.
In a deep bowl, whisk together the eggs, cream, salt, and pepper.
Sprinkle an even amount of cheese and bacon into each cup of the prepared tin. Pour an even amount of egg mixture over the filling.

Bake 20 to 25 minutes, until the eggs puff up and are lightly golden.

Calories 303 Fat 26 Protein 15 Carbs 1.5 Fiber 0 Net carbs 1.5

CHEDDAR CHIVE BAKED AVOCADO EGGS \sServes: 2

2 eggs
2 ounces cheddar cheese, shredded 2 teaspoons heavy cream 1 teasp
fresh chopped chives Sea salt and freshly ground black pepper to tast
avocado, cut in half and pitted (see note) (see note)
Preheat the oven to 425F°.
Combine the eggs, cheddar cheese, cream, half the chives, salt, and pep
in a medium bowl. Beat with a fork until well mixed.
Arrange the avocados in a small rimmed baking dish, cut side up (tl
should be snug so they don't roll around). Pour the egg filling into
centre of each avocado.
Bake 12 minutes, until the filling is lightly golden on top. Serve h
topped with the remaining chives.

Note: Avocado pits vary, so depending on the size, you might need
scoop a little bit extra avocado from the centre with a spoon
accommodate the egg filling.

Calories 257 Fat 22 Protein 13 Carbs 1.3 Fiber 0 Net carbs 1.3

BLUEBERRY ALMOND PANCAKES

Makes: 10 (serving size 2 pancakes) (serving size 2 pancakes)

Aside from the lack of grains, these pancakes are different from the usual in another way: you cover the pan with a lid while they're cooking to ensure that they cook through in the centre.

4 tablespoons butter 2 large eggs
¼ cup almond milk
¼ teaspoon pure vanilla extract ¾ cup almond flour 1 tablespoon flax meal 1 teaspoon baking powder 1 packet stevia powder ¼ teaspoon sea salt ¼ teaspoon allspice (optional) (optional) ¾ cup blueberries, frozen or fresh Butter, to cook the pancakes
In a small bowl, whisk the butter, eggs, almond milk, and vanilla. Whisk in the flour, flax meal, baking powder, stevia, salt, and allspice until well blended. Fold in the blueberries.
Heat a nonstick skillet over medium heat. It's ready to use when a few drops of water dance across the surface. Melt a pat of butter in the pan. Drop scant ¼ cupfuls of batter into the skillet, spreading out into thin circles (they'll puff up). Cover the pan with a lid and cook 1 to 2 minutes until air bubbles appear on top and batter looks a little dry. Flip, and cook until cooked through and golden underneath, about 2 minutes more. Serve hot.

Note: Leftover pancakes may be layered between parchment paper, wrapped in plastic film and stored in the freezer for up to 1 month. Heat them straight from the freezer in a 350ºF oven for 8 to 10 minutes.

Calories 114 Fat 10 Protein 3.9 Carbs 3.9 Fiber 1.4 Net carbs 2.5

TOAD IN A HOLE

Serves: 2

4 sausages de porc (spicy or sweet) 1/3 cup blanched almond flour, fin
tblsp arrowroot powder Almond milk (six tablespoons) a quarter-cup
heavy cream 14 teaspoon salt 1 egg
Preheat the oven to 350°F and place an 8-inch cast-iron pan on the mid
rack. Preheat the oven to 400 degrees Fahrenheit.
In a skillet, brown the sausages. Cook for 12 to 15 minutes, flipping on
until well browned.
In a medium mixing bowl, combine the almond flour, arrowroot, almo
milk, cream, egg, and salt. Whisk until everything is thoroughly combin
Pour the batter into the heated pan after the sausages have been brown
Return the pan to the oven and bake for 20 to 25 minutes, or until puf
up and brown. Serve right away.

376 calories, 28 grammes of fat, 16.3 grammes of protein, 16.2 gramm
of fibre, and 13.8 grammes of net carbohydrates

1 SERVING BERRY BREAKFAST SHAKE

14 cup mixed frozen berries 12 CUP HEAVY COOKER'S CREAM
cup almond or coconut milk 1 tbsp butter made from almonds 12 teaspo
lemon juice, freshly squeezed MCT oil (one tablespoon) (optional)
Add all the ingredients to a blender bowl.

Blend until smooth.
Serve right away.

900 calories, 80 grammes of fat, and 80 grammes of protein
Carbohydrates: 10 Carbohydrates: 18 Fiber: 5 Net Carbohydrates: 13

2 SERVINGS CHEDDAR, SPINACH, AND MUSHROOM OMELET

Sure, this falls under the breakfast category, but omelettes are also a wonderful lunch or supper option, so keep this dish in mind as you plan your week's menu.

2 tsp olive oil (extra virgin) 2 cups baby spinach, packed 3 ounces white button mushrooms, sliced to taste with sea salt 6 big eggs, gently beaten 4 ounces cheddar cheese, shredded Handful of fresh parsley, chopped

1 teaspoon oil, heated in an 8-inch nonstick pan over medium-high heat until shimmering Toss in the mushrooms. Cook for 3 to 4 minutes, stirring the pan a few times, until the mushrooms are brown. Season with salt and pepper after adding the spinach. Cook for 1 to 2 minutes, or until the spinach is slightly wilted. Place the veggies in a mixing bowl. Set aside after adding the parsley.

In the same skillet, heat the remaining teaspoon of oil. Season the eggs with salt and pepper before pouring them into the pan. Cook until the edges of the eggs are set, without disturbing them. Lift the edges of the egg with a rubber spatula while tilting the pan to allow any uncooked egg to slip beneath and cook. Half of the eggs should be covered in the veggie mixture. On top, grate the cheese. To make a half moon, fold the plain egg over the half with the veggies. Cook for a further minute. Serve right away.

500 calories, 38 grammes of fat, 34 grammes of protein, 5 grammes fibre, and 4 grammes of net carbohydrates

LUNCH

Lettuce Wraps with Bacon, Avocado, and Turkey Sesame Zoodles wit Kick
Stuffed Peppers from Italy
Salad of Warm Spinach and Roast Chicken with Bacon Vinaigre
Chicken Salad Caesar with Crispy Parmesan
Ranch Dipping Sauce for Buffalo Chicken Wings Lollipops with bac and shrimp
Avocado & Shrimp Pork-Fried Cauliflower Couscous Cobb Salad

LETTUCE WRAPS WITH BACON, AVOCADO, AND TURKI
SERVES 2

Making a batch of bacon and storing it in the refrigerator allows for qu weekday lunches. It just needs a short heating in a skillet to crisp up. lieu of the turkey, you may use leftover roast chicken.

2 curled kale leaves mayonnaise, 1 tablespoon 4 cooked bacon slice: pitted and sliced avocado 4 turkey slices
Place each kale leaf on a chopping board. Using the mayonnaise, coat chicken. Layer two pieces of bacon, half of the avocado slices, and t

slices of turkey on half of each leaf. Starting with the filled end, roll up. Enjoy.

510 calories 44 g fat, 17 g protein, 14.6 g fibre, 7.3 g net carbohydrates

2 SERVINGS SPICY SESAME ZOODLES

My favourite lunch used to be cold sesame noodles. I'm using zucchini noodles instead of spaghetti (Zoodles, here). To balance out the richness of the almond butter, the sauce usually includes a sweetener. I've left it out here, but you can add 12 packets of stevia to the dressing as you mix it up in the bowl if you want.

14 cup creamy almond butter 12 lime 1 teaspoon of soy sauce 1 tblsp sesame seed oil 12 teaspoon chilli flakes (red) to taste with sea salt 12 cup red cabbage, shredded Fresh cilantro leaves and stems in a handful chopped 1/3 cup sliced almonds 2 scallions, chopped Zoodles are a kind of noodle that is (here)
In a large mixing basin, squeeze the lime.
In a mixing bowl, combine the almond butter, soy sauce, sesame oil, and chilli flakes.
Season with salt and pepper. Whisk until everything is thoroughly combined.
In a large mixing bowl, combine the cabbage, cilantro, onions, almonds, and Zoodles. Toss to evenly coat. Serve right away, or refrigerate for a few minutes before serving.

507 calories

Carbs 14 Fiber 6.8 Net carbs 7.2 Fat 47.6 Protein 12.9 Carbs 14 Fiber 6.8

STUFFED ITALIAN PEPPERS
2 people

1 tbsp olive oil (extra virgin) 8 oz. beef (ground) freshly ground bl:
pepper and sea salt 1 sliced garlic clove 1 cup tomato sauce (slov
simmered) (here) 12 teaspoon basil (dried) 12 teaspoon oregano, dry 1 q
couscous de cauliflower (here) 4 oz. mozzarella shredded 2 bell pepp
red

Heat the oil in a medium skillet until it shimmers. Add the beef and br
up any pieces with a fork (you want little bits of meat). Salt & pepper
taste. Cook until the meat is well browned. Transfer to a bowl witl
slotted spoon and set aside.

In the same pan, add the garlic. Sauté for 1 minute, or until aromatic.

Return the meat to the pan and stir in the tomato sauce, basil, and oregar
Salt & pepper to taste. Reduce the heat to low and continue to cook fo
minutes.

Preheat the oven to 375 degrees Fahrenheit.

While the oven preheats, remove the beef filling from the heat and
aside to cool somewhat.

In a mixing bowl, combine the cauliflower couscous and half of
mozzarella.

Scoop out the seeds from the bell peppers by slicing off the tops. Spc
the meat filling into the peppers in an even layer. In an 8-inch loaf p.
arrange the peppers. The remaining mozzarella should be sprinkled on tc
Bake for 35–40 minutes, or until the peppers are tender and the cheese
golden brown. Serve immediately.

574 calories 40.2 g fat 36.8 g protein 17.9 g fibre 4.2 g net carbohydra
13.7 g

WARM SPINACH & ROAST CHICKEN SALAD WITH BACON VINAIGRETTE

Serves: 2

Most people smash cold bacon onto a hot skillet and then duck for shelter. Adding cold bacon to a cold pan (brilliant, right?) is the simplest method to prevent this. The drippings are used to make a delicious dressing for what seems to be a basic salad. Leftover chicken from the Bone Broth or the Smoky Butter Roasted Chicken may also be used in this recipe.

4 bacon slices 1 crushed garlic clove a couple of tablespoons Mustard dijon red wine vinegar, 2 tblsp. Salt

black pepper, freshly ground 2 cups cooked chicken, diced or shredded 4 cups baby spinach, packed

In a chilly 8-inch skillet, cook the bacon over medium-high heat. Cook, flipping once, till crisp all over. Place on a platter lined with paper towels.

Add the garlic to the same pan. Sauté for 1 minute, or until aromatic. Garlic should be discarded. Remove the pan from the heat and mix in the mustard and vinegar. Salt & pepper to taste. Reduce the heat to a low setting in the skillet. Stir in the chicken and simmer for 1 to 2 minutes, or until warmed through. Remove the skillet from the heat, add the spinach, and divide the salad into two shallow dishes right away. Enjoy right now.

489 calories Carbohydrates 2.9 Fiber 1.3 Net carbs 1.6 Fat 32 Protein 43.8 Carbs 2.9 Fiber 1.3

2 SERVINGS CHICKEN CAESAR SALAD WITH PARMESAN CRISPS

For a variety of reasons, this salad is a favourite. For starters, it make use of leftover roast chicken from this dish. If you don't have any leftover roast chicken, you may use store-bought rotisserie chicken (keep to the herb- or plain-roasted varieties, since they're less likely t include added sweeteners). For hectic weekdays, it's also a simple lunch to bring.

a quarter cup of mayonnaise 1 clove of garlic

1 teaspoon lemon juice, freshly squeezed 14 tblsp soy sauce 12 teaspoon paste of anchovies 1 tblsp. Parmigiano-Reggiano 14 teaspo mustard (Dijon) 1 bunch chopped romaine hearts 2 CUP REMANEN Chicken roasted in a smoky butter sauce 6 Crisps de Parmesan (here)

In a blender, combine the mayonnaise, garlic, lemon juice, soy sauce anchovy paste, Parmesan, and mustard. Blend the dressing until it is smooth and creamy.

Combine the lettuce and chicken in a large mixing basin. Toss in hal of the dressing until evenly covered. Serve with Parmesan Crisps as a garnish. Serve right away.

321 calories Protein 29 Fat 12.4 Carbohydrates 2.8 Fiber 1 Net Carbohydrates 1.8

2 SERVINGS BUFFALO CHICKEN WINGS WITH RANCH DIPPING SAUCE

1 teaspoon powdered baking soda a quarter teaspoon of garlic powder 12 tsp. black pepper, plus more if necessary 14 teaspoon salt, plus more if necessary 8 pieces of chicken wings (wing and drum) 2 tblsp. butter, melted a quarter cup of spicy sauce (preferably one without added sugars) 14 cup ranch dressing (homemade) (here)

Preheat the oven to 375 degrees Fahrenheit. Brush an 11-by-17-inch baking sheet generously with olive oil.

In a large mixing bowl, combine the baking powder, garlic powder, pepper, salt, and 1 tablespoon water. Toss in the chicken until it is well covered. Arrange the chicken on the prepared pan in a single layer. Bake for 20 to 25 minutes, or until golden brown on both sides, flipping halfway through.

In a small mixing dish, combine the butter and spicy sauce. Pour the sauce over the chicken, swirling to ensure that it is well covered. Preheat the oven to 400 degrees Fahrenheit. Bake for another 10 to 15 minutes, or until crispy, rotating halfway through.

With the Homemade Ranch Dressing, serve the chicken wings hot.

310 calories Carbohydrates 2.4 Fiber 0.1 Net carbs 2.3 Fat 26.3 Protein 16.3 Carbs 2.4 Fiber 0.1

2 SERVINGS BACON & SHRIMP LOLLIPOPS

This twist on surf and turf is ideal for a party, so have this dish on ha
for when you're hosting or visiting a friend.

6 slices of bacon (thin-cut works best) 6 shelled and deveined large
shrimp 2 skewers (wooden or metal)

To prevent splinters, soak wooden skewers in water for 2 hours befo
using.

Preheat your oven's broiler on high.

Wrap one slice of bacon around one shrimp to fully cover it (picture
looping a piece of ribbon around a ring). Using the leftover bacon an
shrimp, repeat the process.

Add three pieces to each skewer and slide the skewer lengthwise
through the shrimp (instead of right through the center). Place on a
rimmed baking sheet.

Broil for 4 to 5 minutes, or until golden brown. Broil for another 4 to
minutes, until cooked through. Serve immediately.

Calories: 410 Fat: 34 Protein: 25 Carbs: 1 Fiber: 0 Net Carbs: 1
Calories: 410 Fat: 34 Protein: 25 Carbs: 1 Fiber:

AVOCADO & SHRIMP 2 SERVINGS COBB SALAD

8 big peeled and deveined shrimp 10 grape tomatoes, halved 1 head
Boston lettuce, chopped 1 romaine heart, chopped 4 hard-boiled eggs

sliced in half 4 cooked bacon pieces, crumbled 14 cup Easy Homemade Vinaigrette 1 avocado, pitted and chopped (here)

Fill a 2-quart saucepan halfway with water and bring to a boil over high heat to cook the shrimp. Toss in the shrimp. Remove the saucepan from the heat and cover it. Allow 10 minutes to pass. To halt the cooking process, drain the shrimp and place them in a basin of cold water; leave aside.

Between two shallow bowls, arrange the lettuces, tomatoes, eggs, bacon, avocado, and shrimp. Drizzle the dressing over everything. Serve right away.

838 calories

Carbs 17.9 Fiber 9.5 Net carbs 8.4 Fat 69.6 Protein 40 Carbs 17.9 Fiber 9.5

PORK-FRIED CAULIFLOWER COUSCOUS

Serves: 2

This is a great way to use up extra Cauliflower Couscous (here) (her
In fact, it's a great reason to make the Cauliflower Couscous, so y
can reap the rewards of leftovers—just be sure to make it at least a c
in advance, since it needs to be cold to work best in this dish.

2 teaspoons olive oil 2 eggs, beaten\sSea salt and freshly ground bla
pepper 2 boneless pork chops, diced 1 tablespoon sesame oil
teaspoon freshly grated ginger 1 garlic clove, chopped fine 3 cups cc
cooked Cauliflower Couscous 3 tablespoons soy sauce 2 to 3 scallio
chopped

Heat 1 teaspoon of the olive oil in a deep skillet over medium-hi
heat until shimmering. Add the eggs, and cook, stirring, until cook
through, about 1 minute. Transfer to a small bowl.

Increase the heat to high, and add another teaspoon of olive oil to
pan. Add the pork, and sauté until golden and cooked through, 2 t
minutes. Transfer to the bowl with the eggs.

Heat the sesame oil in the same skillet. Add the ginger and garl
Sauté until fragrant, 15 to 30 seconds. Add the Cauliflower Cousco
making sure to break up any clumps. Stir in the soy sauce a
scallions. Add the pork and egg back to the pan. Sauté until t
Cauliflower Couscous is heated through, 1 to 2 minutes. Serve hot.

Calories 342 Fat 29.5 Protein 16.6 Carbs 5.8 Fiber 1.1 Net carbs 4.7

DINNER

Kimchi Pork Lettuce Cups Thai Turkey Burgers
BBQ Flank Steak and Cabbage Slaw Beef Bolognese\sSmoky Butter
Roasted Chicken Sheet-Pan Chicken Fajita Bowls Almond-Crusted
Salmon Patties Swedish Meatballs
Magic Keto Pizza

KIMCHI PORK LETTUCE CUPS \sServes: 2

This Thai-inspired dish packs a punch of flavour. To eat it, scoop up some of the pork filling with a lettuce leaf, roll it up, and dig in. For a different twist, you can nix the lettuce and serve the filling tossed with zoodles.

2 teaspoons extra virgin olive oil 1 garlic clove, chopped fine 8 ounces ground pork Handful of fresh cilantro, chopped ½ cup kimchi, chopped fine 1 teaspoon fish sauce (Red Boat fish sauce has no added sugar) (Red Boat fish sauce has no added sugar) 1½ teaspoons soy sauce Sea salt to taste
1 small head Boston lettuce, leaves removed, rinsed and patted dry Lime wedges, for garnish Fresh mint, for garnish
In a 10-inch skillet, heat the oil over medium-high heat until shimmering. Add the garlic, and sauté until lightly golden, 1 to 2 minutes. Add the pork, using a fork to break up any large chunks. Add the cilantro, kimchi, fish sauce, and soy sauce. Season with salt. Reduce heat to medium-low. Continue cooking, stirring every couple of minutes, until the pork is completely cooked through, 7 to 9

minutes.

Meanwhile, arrange the lettuce leaves on a platter.

Spoon the cooked pork filling over the lettuce leaves. Garnish w
lime wedges and fresh mint. Serve immediately.

Calories 322 Fat 24.3 Protein 19.7 Carbs 6.8 Fiber 2.6 Net carbs 4.2

THAI TURKEY BURGERS \sServes: 2

These burgers pack a punch of flavour, in all the good ways. If you
got some carbs to spare and are really craving a bun for them, make
Easy Keto Bread here to serve them on. The Zucchini Fries here ar
must!

12 ounces ground turkey 1 garlic clove
1 teaspoon fresh grated ginger Handful of fresh cilantro, stems a
leaves chopped fine 2 teaspoons red curry paste ½ teaspoon sea s
plus more to taste 4 teaspoons mayonnaise ½ teaspoon Dijon mustar
teaspoons extra virgin olive oil Freshly ground black pepper 2 roma
heart leaves or curly kale leaves

In a medium bowl, add the turkey, garlic, ginger, half of the chopp
cilantro, chilli paste, and salt. Mix well. Divide the mixture into
equal portions, and shape into flat 4-inch patties.

In a small bowl, mix together the mayonnaise, Dijon, and remaini
cilantro.

Season with salt and pepper.

Heat the oil in a medium skillet over medium-high heat. Add t
burgers, and cook until browned underneath, 4 to 5 minutes. Flip, a
continue cooking until browned on the other side and cooked throug
4 to 5 minutes more.

Wrap each burger in a lettuce leaf to serve.

Calories 451 Fat 29 Protein 45.5 Carbs 1.8 Fiber 0.8 Net carbs 1

BBQ FLANK STEAK & CABBAGE SLAW

Serves: 4

Although butter may seem strange in a BBQ sauce, it produces a thic
rich-bodied sauce and adds additional fat to a lean cut of meat.

a quarter cup of ketchup (a no-sugar-added variety, such as Primal
Kitchen) 2 teaspoons melted butter 1 teaspoon mustard (Dijon) 12 ts
onion powder 12 TBS WORCESTERSHIRE SAUCE 12 teaspoon
black pepper, freshly ground, plus more as required to taste with sea
salt
a flank steak weighing 112 pounds a quarter cup of mayonnaise
1 tablespoon vinegar (apple cider) a quarter teaspoon of celery seed 2
cups cabbage, shredded
Preheat your oven's broiler to high and place a rack beneath the broil
plate.
Whisk together the ketchup, butter, mustard, onion powder,
Worcestershire sauce, and black pepper in a small bowl to combine.
On a rimmed sheet pan, place the meat. Apply the sauce over the
whole surface, including the top and bottom. Cook for 5 to 7 minutes
or until the top is well browned. Cook for another 5 to 7 minutes, or
until desired doneness is reached. Allow 5 minutes for resting.
Prepare the slaw in the meanwhile. Whisk together the mayonnaise,
vinegar, and celery seed in a large dish in a small bowl. Salt & peppe
to taste. Stir in the cabbage until it is well combined. Refrigerate unti
ready to use. This may be made up to a day ahead of time.
Using a sharp knife, slice the steak against the grain and serve with
slaw.

Note: If you're planning ahead, you may marinate the steak in a zip-to bag with the sauce in the fridge for 1 to 2 days. Cook exactly as instructed.

392 calories, 25 grammes of fat, 37 grammes of protein, 3 grammes of fibre, and 2 grammes of net carbohydrates

BOLOGNESE WITH BEEF SERVES 4

When starting out on the keto diet, many people miss pasta. Here, the sauce takes centre stage, and after you have a mouthful, you'll understand why. It's great with zoodles, but you could also make an Italian sloppy Joe with it and serve it on Easy Keto Bread (here).

4 thick-cut bacon pieces, chopped Ground beef weighing 112 pounds freshly ground black pepper and sea salt a third of a cup of heavy cream
1 tomato purée can (28 ounces) To serve, zoodles (here) To serve, grated Parmesan cheese (optional)
In a chilled deep skillet, cook the bacon over medium-high heat. Cook, flipping once, till crisp all over. Using a slotted spoon, transfer to a bowl.
In a skillet, crumble the meat. Salt & pepper to taste. Cook, stirring periodically, for 5 to 7 minutes, or until thoroughly browned.
Reduce the heat to a low setting. Add the cream and mix well. Cook, stirring periodically, for approximately 10 minutes, or until the cream has largely evaporated but the meat isn't dry.
Scrape up any browned pieces from the bottom of the pan before adding the tomato purée. Season with salt and pepper. Bring the water to a boil. Reduce the heat to a low setting. Cook, stirring periodically, for 2 to 3 hours (see Note). As required, add a few tablespoons of

water to keep the sauce from sticking to the pan.
Begin making the Zoodles here around 30 minutes before the sauce i
done.
Serve the Bolognese with Pecorino, if preferred, over the zoodles.

Note: Once the tomato purée has been added to the pan, transfer the
sauce to a slow cooker and simmer for 4 to 6 hours on low.

532 calories 36.2 g fat 42.6 g protein 8.4 g fibre 3.7 g net
carbohydrates

4 SERVINGS SMOKY BUTTER ROASTED CHICKEN

When it comes to roast chicken, two things to keep in mind: high hea
is your friend, and you don't need to truss the bird (tie the legs and
wings back). While trussing the chicken looks nice, leaving it alone
enables the heat to flow throughout the chicken, allowing it to cook
quicker and more evenly. Remove the paprika, garlic, and herbs from
the butter for a simplified version of this dish.

6 tablespoons softened butter smoked paprika, 112 teaspoons 1 grate
garlic clove To taste, a handful of fresh flat-leaf parsley, minced sea
salt, and freshly ground black pepper Whole chicken weighing 312
pounds
Preheat the oven to 450 degrees Fahrenheit.
Combine the butter, paprika, garlic, parsley, salt, and pepper in a sma
bowl.
Mix everything together with a fork until everything is thoroughly
combined.
In a roasting pan, place the chicken. Using your hands, rub the butter

mixture all over the surface. Cook for 20 minutes, then pour 1/2 cup of water into the pan's bottom to keep the drippings from burning and create a natural sauce from the juices. Roast for another 40 to 50 minutes, basting every 15 minutes, or until the juices flow clear and an instant-read thermometer inserted in the thigh registers 165 degrees Fahrenheit.

Before slicing the chicken, remove it from the oven and let it aside for 5 to 10 minutes.

614 calories, 51 grammes of fat, 37 grammes of protein, 0.5 grammes of fibre, and 0.5 grammes of net carbohydrates

SHEET-PAN CHICKEN FAJITA BOWLS
Serves: 2

2 to 3 tablespoons melted butter 2 to 3 chicken thighs, skin-on 2 chicl
legs, skin-on taco seasoning (taco seasoning) (taco seasoning) ((be sure
choose one without hidden sweeteners) freshly ground black pepper a
sea salt 1 seeded and sliced poblano pepper 2 chopped garlic cloves 1 tl
olive oil (extra virgin) Couscous with Cauliflower (here) 1 lime, zest
and the rest of the lime, quartered Chopped leaves and stems from a sm
bouquet of fresh cilantro

Preheat the oven to 450 degrees Fahrenheit.

1 to 2 tablespoons butter should be rubbed all over the chicken piec
Place on a 9-by-13-inch rimmed baking sheet in a single layer. Seas
with salt and pepper and a dash of taco spice. Drizzle the olive oil over
poblano and garlic in the pan.

Roast for 15 to 20 minutes, or until the chicken starts to brown. Stir
peppers to coat them in the pan juices. If the pan seems to be too dry, a
a few tablespoons of water. Some of the liquids should be poured over
chicken. Bake for another 15 to 20 minutes, or until an instant-re
thermometer reads 165°F for the chicken.

Meanwhile, make the Cauliflower Couscous according to the instructic
on this page. Stir add the lime zest and half of the cilantro once it I
finished cooking.

Divide the couscous into two broad, shallow dishes to serve. Each pl
should be topped with a chicken leg and thigh, as well as some of
peppers. Using a spoon, drizzle some of the pan juices on top. Finish w
the remaining cilantro and serve!

455 calories, 32 grammes of fat, 36.3 grammes of protein, 6 grammes

fibre, and 3.7 grammes of net carbohydrates

4 SERVINGS ALMOND-CRUSTED SALMON PATTIES

When individuals go keto, they may see an increase in their food expenditures. Using canned salmon offers you more bang for your money while still providing omega-3 and calcium advantages.

2 cans wild pink salmon (6 oz.) 14 teaspoon paprika 1 tablespoon Dijon mustard a handful of chopped fresh flat-leaf parsley a single big egg
To taste, season with sea salt and freshly ground black pepper. 1 c. almond flour coconut oil (two teaspoons)
Combine the salmon, mustard, paprika, parsley, egg, salt, pepper, and 12 cup almond meal in the bowl of a food processor. Pulse the ingredients together until they are coarsely mixed (a few chunks of salmon remaining). Refrigerate for at least 1 hour, preferably overnight, after transferring to a bowl and covering with plastic wrap.
Divide the salmon mixture into 8 even balls when ready to cook. Make patties out of them. Coat them completely with the remaining 12 cup of almond meal. 1 tablespoon coconut oil, melted in a 10-inch nonstick pan over medium heat until shimmering Place the patties in the pan and cook them (you might need to do this in batches, so as to not overcrowd the pan). Cook for 3 to 4 minutes, or until golden underneath. Cook for 3 to 4 minutes longer on the other side, until golden.
Serve immediately.

369 calories 26 g fat, 26 g protein, 26 g carbs, 7 g fibre 3.5 net carbohydrates

2 SERVINGS SWEDISH MEATBALLS

1 pound beef mince a single egg
14 teaspoon freshly grated nutmeg 1 garlic clove, grated 2 tablespo
fresh flat-leaf parsley, chopped a quarter cup of almond flour a qua
teaspoon of salt to taste freshly ground black pepper 2 tablespo
unsalted butter 1 tablespoon mustard (Dijon) (be sure to buy one with
added sugars) a tablespoon of soy sauce 2 teaspoons flour de coco 34
broth (chicken or beef) 12 CUP HEAVY COOKER'S CREAM

Combine the meat, egg, garlic, nutmeg, parsley, almond flour, salt,
pepper in a medium mixing bowl. Stir everything together with y
hands, or a wooden spoon if you like, until everything is thoroug
combined. Form into eight balls.

In an 8-inch skillet, melt the butter over medium-high heat. Toss in
meatballs. Cook for 8 to 10 minutes, turning as needed, until browned
over. Place in a serving dish and put away.

All except 1 tablespoon of the grease in the skillet should be discard
Stir in the mustard, soy sauce, and coconut flour over medium he
scraping off any browned pieces. Add the broth and mix well. Bring
water to a boil. Reduce the heat to a low heat and add the cream. Salt
pepper to taste. Return the meatballs to the pan and simmer for anothe
to 10 minutes, or until the sauce has thickened. Serve immediately.

728 calories, 51 grammes of fat Carbohydrates 8.4 Fiber 2.8 Net carbs
Protein 59.6

MAGIC KETO PIZZA

Serves: 2 to 4

Pizza is one of the foods that many people miss when they go carb-free. As an Italian girl from Brooklyn, I completely understand, and I am extremely happy to share this dish with you. Let's face it: nothing beats a conventional crust, but this crust is really incredible, almost magical. When you hold up a slice that defies gravity and it doesn't flip over, you've passed the true test! The only decision you have to make while you eat it is whether or not to fold it.

CRUST CONTROL
a single egg
6 oz. mozzarella cheese, shredded 4 tablespoons softened butter (broken into pieces) 12 cup blanched, superfine almond flour coconut flour (six tablespoons) 2 tablespoons powdered baking soda a quarter teaspoon of salt

TO MAKE THE PIZZA
34 cup tomato sauce (slowly simmered) (here) 6 oz. mozzarella cheese, shredded Toppings that are keto-friendly

Preheat the oven to 375 degrees Fahrenheit.

In the bowl of a food processor, combine the egg, mozzarella, butter, flours, baking powder, and sea salt to create the crust. Pulse until a rough ball develops. Coconut flour should be gently dusted on a counter. Knead the dough for 30 to 60 seconds, until it becomes smooth, adding additional coconut flour just as required to prevent it from sticking.

Place the dough on a parchment-paper-lined baking sheet. Cover with a second parchment or waxed paper sheet. Make a 1/8-inch thick round

out of the dough. The top layer of parchment should be removed. Pl
the dough on a pizza pan while it is still on the parchment paper. B
for 15 minutes, or until gently browned.

Cover with tomato sauce, leaving a 14- to 12-inch border around
perimeter. Add any preferred toppings and top with the remain
mozzarella cheese. Bake for another 15 to 20 minutes, or until
cheese is melted and bubbling and the crust is crisp. Allow fo
minutes of resting time before slicing and serving.

Place the slices in a nonstick skillet over medium heat to reh
leftovers. Cook until hot, then serve.

Nutritional analysis is per slice. Calories 169 Fat 10 Protein 16 Ca
5.4 Fiber 2 Net carbs 3.4

BEVERAGES & TREATS

Espresso Orange Fat Bombs made with Chia Pudding and Almo
Butter Avocado Mousse Berry Cheesecake Bars with Almond J
Whipped Coconut Cream Bulletproof Mocha Coffee Bulletpr
Mocha Coffee Bulletproof Mocha Coffee Bulletproof Mocha Cof
Bullet Chai with Coconut

2 SERVINGS ORANGE ESPRESSO CHIA PUDDING

I'm convinced there's a chia-pudding plot going on. Every recipe states it should be chilled overnight. I've never had luck with this technique, since chia seeds actually require a full 24 hours to fully absorb the liquids and swell up. So plan ahead when making these. The good news is the recipe can be doubled, and it keeps a few days in the fridge. Make a batch if you like, and enjoy chia pudding all week long.

¾ cup unsweetened almond milk 2 tablespoons espresso or strongly brewed coffee Zest of 1 orange

1 packet stevia powder (optional) (optional) 4 tablespoons white chia seeds 2 tablespoons sliced almonds, toasted

In a small bowl, whisk together the coconut milk, espresso, orange zest, and stevia, if using. Stir in the chia seeds until well mixed.

Divide between two 8-ounce mason jars. Cover with the lid. Chill for at least 24 hours, and up to 2 days. The pudding will keep, covered, for up to 4 days. To serve, top each pudding with half the almonds.

Calories 206 Fat 14.4 Protein 7.2 Carbs 14.9 Fiber 10.1 Net carbs 4.8

CHOCOLATE ALMOND BUTTER CUP FAT BOMBS
Makes: 12 bite-sized pieces (serving size 1 piece) (serving size 1 piece)

6 tablespoons dark chocolate chips (Lily's are sweetened with stevia) 6 tablespoons almond butter 6 tablespoons coconut oil 1 packet stevia powder

Line a 12-cup mini muffin tin with paper liners.

In a small microwave-safe bowl, melt the chocolate chips in 30-second intervals. Pour half into the prepared tin cups. Let cool for 5 minutes.

In a small pot, combine the almond butter and coconut oil over l heat. Cook until melted, stirring together to mix. Stir in the stevia. P an even amount over the chocolate in the paper liners.

Evenly pour the remaining chocolate over the almond butter filling. in the fridge to firm up, at least two hours. Keep refrigerated.

Calories 135 Fat 13.4 Protein 2.2 Carbs 6 Fiber 2.8 Net carbs 3.2

ALMOND JOY AVOCADO MOUSSE \sServes: 2

One of my favourite candy bars in keto dessert form!

1 ripe avocado, pitted and fruit scooped from skin 1 to 2 packets ste powder 2 tablespoons cocoa powder ½ teaspoon vanilla extract 6 t tablespoons coconut milk (depends on size of avocado) (depends size of avocado) 1 tablespoon dark chocolate chips 1 tablespc coconut flakes 1 tablespoon sliced almonds Coconut Whipped Crea to serve (optional; here) (optional; here)

Add the avocado, stevia, cocoa powder, vanilla, and coconut milk the bowl of a food processor.

Pulse until smooth.

Evenly spoon the pudding into 2 small bowls or jars. Top evenly w the chocolate chips, coconut flakes, and almonds. Cover with plas film, and chill for at least 2 hours, until pudding is set. May be ma up to 1 day in advance. Top with Coconut Whipped Cream befo serving, if using.

Calories 268 Fat 37 Protein 263.4 Carbs 22.7 Fiber 13 Net carbs 9.7

BERRY CHEESECAKE BARS
Makes: 8 bars (serving size 1 bar) (serving size 1 bar)

CRUST CONTROL
3 tablespoons butter, melted 1 cup almond flour 1 packet stevia powder

FOR THE FILLING
8 ounces full-fat cream cheese, softened a single egg
2 packets stevia powder 1 teaspoon lemon juice ¼ cup raspberries or blueberries

Preheat the oven to 350ºF.

Line an 8-inch loaf pan with a piece of parchment paper long enough to hang over the sides (this acts as a sling to lift the bars out when done) (this acts as a sling to lift the bars out when done).

To make the crust, combine the butter, almond flour, and stevia in a small bowl. Stir with until mixed, then press into bottom of the prepared baking pan. Bake until set, 7 to 8 minutes. Let cool completely.

To make the filling, combine the cream cheese, egg, stevia, and lemon juice in a medium bowl. Stir with a fork until well blended. Pour over the crust.

Mash the berries lightly with the back of a fork, just to break them up a bit. Scatter over the filling and use a butter knife to swirl them through the cream- cheese mixture.

Bake 15 to 20 minutes, until centre is mostly set (it'll jiggle slightly like Jell- O). Let cool completely, then chill for at least three hours, or overnight, before cutting into 8 even bars.

Calories 229 Fat 21.7 Protein 5.6 Carbs 5.7 Fiber 1.6 Net carbs 4.1

COCONUT WHIPPED CREAM
Makes: 1 cup (serving size 1 tablespoon) (serving size 1 tablespoon)

Making a keto-friendly whipped cream at home is easier than you
think! All it requires is advance planning, since the canned coco
milk needs to be chilled for a full day in order for it to whip proper
It's perfect as a topping for the Almond Joy Avocado Mousse here,
just add some berries and enjoy it as a quick snack. Want to jazz it u
Try adding a dash of cinnamon, 1 teaspoon of cocoa, or some cit
zest before you whip it.

1 can (15 ounces) full-fat, unsweetened coconut milk

24 hours before you plan to make this whipped cream, place the can
coconut milk in the fridge.
The next day, open the can, scoop out the solids and add them to
small bowl (save the remaining coconut water for another use) (sa
the remaining coconut water for another use). Using a handheld mix
whip the coconut solids until fluffy and thickened into a slightly st
cream. Use immediately.

Calories 61 Fat 6.3 Protein 0.6 Carbs 1.4 Fiber 0.6 Net carbs 0.8

MOCHA BULLETPROOF COFFEE

Serves: 1

When you need a quick boost of energy that also leaves you feeling full, bulletproof coffee is the way to go. The butter and MCT oil bulk it up into a satisfying mini-meal. It's a great way to start the day or as an afternoon pick-me- up to keep snacking at bay. Should you want a little sweet touch, you can add ½ packet stevia powder—any more will accentuate coffee's natural bitter notes.

¾ cup hot brewed coffee 2 tablespoons unsalted butter 1 tablespoon MCT oil (optional) (optional) ½ teaspoon cocoa powder ¼ teaspoon cinnamon
Add all the ingredients to a blender bowl. Blend on high for 30 to 60 seconds, until frothy.

Calories 327

Fat 39.4 Protein 0.7 Carbs 0 Fiber 0 Net carbs 0

BULLETPROOF COCONUT CHAI \sServes: 1

Traditional chai is loaded with sugar. This version, a tea relative of the popular bulletproof coffee, delivers all the aromatic flavours plus a boost of energy without providing the cloyingly sweet consequences.

12 ounces hot brewed black tea 2 tablespoons unsalted butter 1 tablespoon MCT oil ¼ cup unsweetened coconut milk ¼ teaspoon cardamom\s¼ teaspoon fresh grated ginger ¼ teaspoon ground clove ½ teaspoon cinnamon

Add all the ingredients to a blender bowl. Blend on high for 30 to 60 seconds, until frothy.

Calories 464 Fat 51 Protein 3.5 Carbs 7 Fiber 1 Net carbs 6

BASICS

Slow-Roasted Chicken-Bone Broth Easy Keto Bread
Slow-Simmered Tomato Sauce Homemade Ranch Dressing Easy Homemade Vinaigrette Homemade Parmesan Crisps Cauliflower Couscous
Zoodles Zucchini Fries

SLOW-ROASTED CHICKEN-BONE BROTH
Makes: about 1 quart

8 chicken thighs, skin-on and bone-in 3 garlic cloves, peeled and smashed 4 celery ribs, cut into 2-inch pieces freshly ground black pepper and sea salt 3 tablespoons extra virgin olive oil Handful of fre

flat-leaf Italian parsley

Preheat your oven to 475°F, with the rack adjusted to the upper centre position.

Arrange the chicken pieces, garlic, and celery in a 9-by-13-inch roasting pan.

Salt & pepper to taste. Roast for 15 minutes.

Drizzle the oil on top. Roast for 15 more minutes.

Add the parsley and pour 6 cups of water into the pan. Roast for 30 more minutes.

Reduce the oven temperature to 275°F. Roast for at least 3 hours and up to 6 hours, adding more water to the pan as needed to keep the chicken covered by about two-thirds. You want the tops to get nicely browned but remain mostly submerged so the meat braises. Taste the broth as it cooks, and add more salt, as needed, according to your tastes.

Using a slotted spoon, transfer the chicken to a plate. Once cooled, remove the meat, and discard the bones. The chicken is perfect as a simple sandwich on Easy Keto Bread (here)—don't forget the mayo! It can also be used in the Cobb Salad here instead of salmon, or the Chicken Caesar Salad here.

Strain the stock, discarding any solids. Let the stock cool completely, then pack in containers, and refrigerate for up to 1 week, or store in the freezer for up to 2 months.

Calories 40 Fat 0.3 Protein 9.4 Carbs 0.6 Fiber 0 Net carbs 0.6
Nutritional analysis is based on one cup.

EASY KETO BREAD

Yes, bread really is possible on keto. Hello, avocado toast! Unlike so many of the bread recipes out there, this one doesn't taste eggy. I really

love the microwave version, but I am including an option to bake the
too. The baked version is lighter in texture, and it must cool complet
before you use it, or it'll crumble. The microwave bread is perfect fo
slicing and toasting when you want bread in less than 2 minutes (no
joke) (no joke). The texture reminds me of crumpets with all the noo
and crannies, and it is lovely split and toasted in a skillet with some
butter (a conventional toaster works too).

2 teaspoons melted butter a single big egg
1 tablespoon water or almond milk 2 tablespoons almond flour 1
tablespoon coconut flour ½ teaspoon baking powder 1/8 teaspoon se
salt

MICROWAVE METHOD

Use a pastry brush to coat the sides and bottoms of two 3½-inch (6-
ounce) or one 5-inch (10-ounce) microwave-safe ramekins with som
of the butter.

In a small bowl, whisk together the egg and water or almond milk.
Whisk in the flours, baking powder, and salt.

Cook on high for 60 to 90 seconds for small breads and 1 to 2 minute
for larger ones, until cooked through (cook small ramekins one at a
time for best results). Test for doneness by gently tapping the centre
with your finger; if it springs back, that means it's cooked through. L
cool for 1 minute. Slide a knife around the inside rim to loosen the
bread. Turn out onto a board. Slice in half and use as you would
sandwich bread.

OVEN METHOD

Preheat the oven to 400°F. Cut out parchment circles to line the botto
of two 3½-inch (6-ounce) or one 5-inch (10-ounce) oven-safe rameki
Generously grease the sides with butter.

In a small bowl, whisk together the egg and water or almond milk.

Whisk in the flours, baking powder, and salt.

Scrape the batter into the prepared ramekin. Bake 12 to 18 minutes, until cooked through. Start checking smaller ones at 10 minutes (a skewer inserted in the centre should come out clean—don't test too soon or you'll deflate the bread). Let cool completely, then slice in half, and use as you would sandwich bread.

Note: The smaller size is great for sliders, while the larger makes a great burger bun.

Calories 194

Fat 18 Protein 5.5 Carbs 4.5 Fiber 2 Net carbs 2.5 Nutritional analysis based on one small bread.

SLOW-SIMMERED TOMATO SAUCE
Approximately 312 cup (serving size 12 cup)

San Marzano tomatoes in a can (28 ounces) Whole and peeled tomatoes 14 cup extra virgin olive oil 3 garlic cloves, crushed 12 teaspoon basil (dried) season with salt to taste

In a blender, puree the tomatoes until smooth. If you want a chunkier sauce, you may just smash them with your hands into the pan.

In a deep pan, combine the tomatoes, garlic, olive oil, basil, and salt. Cook for 45 minutes on low heat setting, uncovered. It'll start simmering strongly about 15 to 20 minutes into the cooking time—don't worry, that's normal.

The sauce is ready to serve after 45 minutes, or you can transfer it to a jar, cool fully, and store in the refrigerator for up to 3 days or the freezer for up to 2 months.

88 calories 8.3 g fat, 1 g protein, 4.3 g carbohydrates, 2.2 g fibre, 2.1 g net

carbs

RANCH DRESSING MADE AT HOME
Approximately 1 cup (serving size 1 tablespoon)

a quarter-cup of mayonnaise a quarter-cup of sour cream 2 tsp lemon juice, freshly squeezed apple cider vinegar, 1 teaspoon a handful of chopped fresh chives

In a medium mixing bowl, combine the mayonnaise, sour cream, lemon juice, and vinegar with 2 tablespoons of water. Add the chives and mix well. Salt & pepper to taste. Refrigerate for up to a week before serving. Before each usage, give it a good shake.

60 calories 6.2 g fat, 0.6 g protein, 0.6 g carbohydrates, 0.6 g fibre, 0 g net carbs

VINAIGRETTE MADE AT HOME

34 cup (about) (serving size 1 tablespoon)

It occurs all the time. We're all busy, and packing a lunch on some mornings is difficult. Keep a bottle of this homemade salad dressing in your desk drawer and you'll always be able to put up a keto-friendly lunch from the salad bar. To avoid hidden sweeteners, stick to basic foods that are raw or steamed, and add a few hard-boiled eggs to provide fat and protein. (Don't worry about the herbs deteriorating at room temperature; the dressing contains enough vinegar to keep them fresh.)

12 CUP EXTRA VIRGIN EXTRA VIRGIN EXTRA VIRGIN EX a quarter cup of red wine vinegar 2 tablespoons mustard (whole grain) herbs of your choice, chopped (chives, cilantro, parsley, scallions) To taste, season with sea salt and freshly ground black pepper. In a mason jar, combine all of the ingredients. Close the lid firmly. Shake until everything is thoroughly combined. It will keep for up to a month at room temperature. Before each usage, give it a good shake.

83 calories 9.5 g fat, 0.1 g protein, 0.1 g

carbohydrates, 0.1 g fibre, 0 g net carbs

PARMESAN CRISPS MADE AT HOME SERVES 12

These easy-to-make cheddar crisps will satisfy your chip need. Only one item and less than ten minutes are required. They also make fantastic salad croutons (see the Chicken Caesar Salad with Parmesan Crisps here).

Pecorino-Locatelli cheese, finely grated

METHOD IN THE OVEN
Preheat the oven to 350 degrees Fahrenheit. Use a silicon mat or parchment paper to line a sheet pan.
Spread the cheese in 12 mounds (approximately 2 tablespoons each) on the baking sheet, allowing 1 inch between them so they can spread.
5–7 minutes in the oven, until brown and bubbling. They'll be mushy when they come out of the oven, but they'll crisp up quickly after they've cooled.

METHOD FOR THE STOVE-TOP

Over medium-low heat, heat a nonstick skillet. Fill the skillet with heaps of cheese (about 2 tablespoons each). Cook for approximately 2 minutes, or until the cheese has melted and become golden around the edges. To loosen and turn them, use an offset spatula. Cook for another 1 to 2 minutes. Transfer to a platter and let aside to crisp up for a few minutes.

38 calories 2.5 g fat, 3.5 g protein, 0.3 g fibre, and 0.3 g net carbohydrates

2   SERVINGS   CAULIFLOWER COUSCOUS

After just one bite, you'll be wondering where this simple side has been all your life. The trick is to keep stirring the cauliflower couscous while it cooks to let the water evaporate as it comes out of the cauliflower; otherwise, it would steam and get mushy.

Cauliflower florets alone, little head (save stems for another use) 2 tablespoons unsalted butter to taste with sea salt

In a food processor, combine the florets. Pulse until the mixture is broken down into fine couscous-like pieces.

1 tablespoon butter, melted in a deep nonstick pan Cook, stirring frequently, until the cauliflower is soft, about 5 to 7 minutes. Add the remaining tablespoon of butter and mix well. Salt & pepper to taste. Before serving, fluff with a fork.

116 calories 11.8 g fat, 1.3 g protein, 2.6 g carbohydrates, 1.4 g fibre, 1.2 g net carbs

ZOODLES

Serves: 2

It may seem ridiculous to have a zoodles recipe that just calls for spiralizing zucchini, but there's more to creating them than that.

zucchini (medium) 2 tablespoons unsalted butter to taste with sea salt Spiralizer is a unique piece of equipment.

Slice the zucchini into thin noodles using a spiralizer. On the counter, place a clean kitchen towel. Sprinkle a little salt on the zucchini strands and spread them out on the cloth. This aids in the removal of surplus water. Dry the noodles with a paper towel.

Melt the butter in a large pan over medium heat. Toss in the zoodles. 1 minute of sautéing To keep the texture, you'll want to keep them a bit raw. They're ready to eat, serve as a side dish, or incorporate into another recipe like Spicy Sesame Zoodles (here).

107 calories 11.6 g fat, 0.8 g protein, 0.8 g fibre, 0.3 g net carbohydrates

2 SERVINGS ZUCCHINI FRIES

You don't have to give up fries because of low-carb zucchini!

1 zucchini, medium
12 cup finely shredded Parmesan cheese
1 egg, beaten

Preheat the oven to 425°F and place the lowest rack in the oven. Using parchment paper, line a rimmed baking sheet.
Ends of zucchini should be trimmed. Cut the zucchini in half lengthwise, then into 14-inch-thick strips on each side. Each piece of zucchini should be dipped in the egg, shaken off any excess, and then dipped in the cheese. Arrange the zucchini on the prepared pan in a single layer.
Bake for 25 to 30 minutes, or until crisp and brown, flipping halfway through.
Serve immediately.

120 calories, 8 grammes of fat, and 8 grammes of protein 10.9 Carbs 1.1 Fiber 0.1 Net Carbs 10.9 Carbs 1.1 Fiber 0.1 Net Carbs 10.9 Carbs 1.1

PART III
RESOURCES

MEAL PLANNER 1: MEALS FROM NOON TO 6PM ONLY

Use the following pages to plan what you are going to eat over the ne. 4 weeks.

DAY 1

Morning	KETO
Noon	KETO
Before 6pm	KETO

DAY 2

Morning	KETO
Noon	KETO
Before 6pm	KETO

DAY 3

Morning	KETO
Noon	KETO
Before 6pm	KETO

DAY 4

Morning	KETO
Noon	KETO
Before 6pm	KETO

DAY 5

Morning	KETO
Noon	KETO
Before 6pm	KETO

DAY 6

Morning	KETO
Noon	KETO
Before 6pm	KETO

DAY 7

Morning	KETO
Noon	KETO
Before 6pm	KETO

DAY 8

Morning	FAST
Noon	KETO
Midday Snack	KETO
Before 6pm	KETO

DAY 9

Morning	FAST
Noon	KETO
Midday Snack	KETO
Before 6pm	KETO

DAY 10

Morning	FAST
Noon	KETO
Midday Snack	KETO
Before 6pm	KETO

DAY 11

Morning	FAST
Noon	KETO
Midday Snack	KETO
Before 6pm	KETO

DAY 12

Morning	FAST
Noon	KETO
Midday Snack	KETO
Before 6pm	KETO

DAY 13

Morning	FAST
Noon	KETO
Midday Snack	KETO
Before 6pm	KETO

DAY 14

Morning	KETO
Noon	KETO
Midday Snack	None
Before 6pm	KETO

DAY 15

Morning	FAST
Noon	KETO
Midday Snack	KETO
Before 6pm	KETO

DAY 16

Morning	FAST
Noon	KETO
Midday Snack	KETO
Before 6pm	KETO

DAY 17

Morning	FAST
Noon	KETO
Midday Snack	KETO
Before 6pm	KETO

DAY 18

Morning	FAST
Noon	KETO
Midday Snack	KETO
Before 6pm	KETO

DAY 19

Morning	FAST
Noon	KETO
Midday Snack	KETO
Before 6pm	KETO

DAY 20

Morning	FAST
Noon	KETO
Midday Snack	KETO
Before 6pm	KETO

DAY 21

Morning	KETO
Noon	KETO
Midday Snack	None
Before 6pm	KETO

DAY 22

Morning	FAST
Noon	KETO
Midday Snack	KETO
Before 6pm	KETO

DAY 23

Morning	FAST
Noon	KETO
Midday Snack	KETO
Before 6pm	KETO

DAY 24

Morning	FAST
Noon	KETO
Midday Snack	KETO
Before 6pm	KETO

DAY 25

Morning	FAST
Noon	KETO
Midday Snack	KETO
Before 6pm	KETO

DAY 26

Morning	FAST
Noon	KETO
Midday Snack	KETO
Before 6pm	KETO

DAY 27

Morning	FAST
Noon	KETO
Midday Snack	KETO
Before 6pm	KETO

DAY 28

Morning	KETO
Noon	KETO
Midday Snack	None
Before 6pm	KETO

MEAL PLANNER 2: ALTERNATE INTERMITTENT FASTING

DAY 1

Morning	KETO
Noon	KETO
Before 6pm	KETO

DAY 2

Morning	KETO
Noon	KETO
Before 6pm	KETO

DAY 3

Morning	KETO
Noon	KETO
Before 6pm	KETO

DAY 4

Morning	KETO
Noon	KETO
Before 6pm	KETO

DAY 5

Morning	KETO
Noon	KETO
Before 6pm	KETO

DAY 6

Morning	KETO
Noon	KETO
Before 6pm	KETO

DAY 7

Morning	KETO
Noon	KETO
Before 6pm	KETO

DAY 8

Morning	KETO
Noon	KETO
Before 6pm	FAST

DAY 9

Morning	KETO
Noon	KETO
Before 6pm	FAST

DAY 10

Morning	FAST
Noon	KETO
Before 6pm	KETO

DAY 11

Morning	KETO
Noon	KETO
Before 6pm	FAST

DAY 12

Morning	FAST
Noon	KETO
Before 6pm	KETO

DAY 13

Morning	KETO
Noon	KETO
Before 6pm	KETO

DAY 14

Morning	KETO
Noon	KETO
Before 6pm	FAST

DAY 15

Morning	FAST
Noon	KETO
Before 6pm	KETO

DAY 16

Morning	KETO
Noon	KETO
Before 6pm	FAST

DAY 17

Morning	FAST
Noon	KETO
Before 6pm	KETO

DAY 18

Morning	KETO
Noon	KETO
Before 6pm	FAST

DAY 19

Morning	FAST
Noon	KETO
Before 6pm	KETO

DAY 20

Morning	KETO
Noon	KETO
Before 6pm	KETO

DAY 21

Morning	KETO
Noon	KETO
Before 6pm	FAST

DAY 22

Morning	FAST
Noon	KETO
Before 6pm	KETO

DAY 23

Morning	KETO
Noon	KETO
Before 6pm	FAST

DAY 24

Morning	FAST
Noon	KETO
Before 6pm	KETO

DAY 25

Morning	KETO
Noon	KETO
Before 6pm	FAST

DAY 26

Morning	FAST
Noon	KETO
Before 6pm	KETO

DAY 27

Morning	KETO
Noon	KETO